Praise for *Writing Together*

"*Writing Together* is a unique dual-memoir that guides readers to pen their own creative journeys. A real gift. It's a beautiful model of the kind of friendship that can make us better people and make the world a better place."

PARKER J. PALMER Author of *Let Your Life Speak, A Hidden Wholeness,* and *On the Brink of Everything*

"Often we think of writing as a solitary act, but *Writing Together* celebrates the intimacy, joy and connection that are possible when we choose to share in this creative process—how beautifully we might grow together, even as we grow ourselves. I love how curiosity, open questions, and authenticity are at the heart of this book. It's an inspiration for poetry lovers, friends and writers of all kinds."

ROSEMERRY WAHTOLA TROMMER Poet and author of *The Unfolding* and *All the Honey*

"*Writing Together* is a love story about a friendship. I love reading the authors' stories, and I am inspired by the ways their writing allowed them to see their hidden wholeness. I can't wait to follow their suggestions for my own writing."

SALLY Z. HARE Endowed Professor Emerita, Coastal Carolina University, and author of *The ElderGarten*

"While writing is often a solitary feat, this book proves that there is another way. It models a rare alchemy of inner work, writing, and friendship. Over a year of Zoom calls, Penny and Darcy engaged in courageously writing their stories, both deepening their friendship while also befriending their unknown selves. Their narratives served as a siren call to my own stories that lie buried and long to see the light of day. I can hardly wait to try this process with a close friend."

CARYL CASBON Author of *The Everywhere Oracle* and *Side by Side: The Sacred Art of Couples Aging with Wisdom and Love*

"Ever want a writing buddy but felt insecure or vulnerable about what that could look or be like? In *Writing Together*, Penny and Darcy craft a journey into what the process of being in trustworthy relationship while writing together can look like that is grounded, bounded and creates space for two people to express themselves deeply while being met with open honest questions and the opportunity for reflection rather than critique. Weaving in their own experiences of life with a trustworthy process for writing together—not as a perfectionistic pursuit of prose but as a process for connection, meaning-making and wholeness—Darcy and Penny chart a path that many others could use, whether they ever decide to publish their work or not. I only wish I had had this book a couple years ago, when a friend and distinguished author offered to write together—and, despite having been published myself many times, I felt too intimidated to do it. Thanks to this book, I have a process I can use to try again."

SOMAVA SAHA, MD, MS President & CEO, WE in the World Institute; Faculty, Harvard Medical School

"Penny and Darcy have co-authored a remarkable book. I have savored it and believe it will change my life."

LORNA LYNN, MD Vice President, Medical Assessment Engagement, American Board of Internal Medicine

"Writing is a generally a solitary pursuit, but Penny Williamson and Darcy Shaw demonstrate that writing can be a shared process of deepening friendship and exploration of life's important questions. *Writing Together* is a lovely book, filled with the search for meaning rooted in friendship, that can transform the solitariness of reading and writing into a shared journey of discovery."

DAVID R. KOPACZ, MD Author of *Caring for Self & Others* and *Becoming Medicine*

"Deeply and remarkably one of the most moving pieces of collective work that I have read in some time. When I finished *Writing Together*, I realized I had a smile on my face and tears in my eyes. I was swept away—taken up and held by the storytelling, by the deep sharing between two friends grounded in truth-telling, mutuality, and humanity. I didn't want the book to end.

"The generosity, graciousness, and respect that Darcy and Penny extend to each other—and now to us, the readers—are both inspiring and instructive. They show us not only how to write, but how to live and love. How to honor our buried and untold stories, and how to harness them for fulfillment and growth as we move through the stages and ages of life."

CINDY L. ADAMS Co-author of *Skills for Communicating in Veterinary Medicine*, Emeritus, Professor of Veterinary Medicine, University of Calgary

"*Writing Together* is more than a guide to creative practice; it is a heartfelt tribute to the transformative power of friendship and shared expression. Williamson and Shaw offer an inspiring example of how writing can nurture connection, purpose, and emotional resilience.

"Williamson draws on her experience in leadership and coaching to bring clarity, courage, and emotional depth to the narrative. Shaw, with his background in veterinary medicine and education, brings a thoughtful and observant voice, blending analytical perspective with honest introspection. Together, their collaborative storytelling creates a sincere, balanced, and enriching reading experience."

SUZIE HOUSLEY Midwest Book Review

Writing Together

Writing Together

a year of meaning-making and friendship

PENNY WILLIAMSON
DARCY SHAW

CREATIVE
COURAGE
PRESS

Courage to Lead® and the Courage & Renewal® approach are registered trademarks of the Center for Courage & Renewal.

Creative Courage Press, LLC (Palisade, CO)
www.CreativeCouragePress.com

ISBN 978-1-959921-06-6 (paperback)
ISBN 978-1-959921-07-3 (ebook)
First edition (all formats): 2025

Library of Congress Cataloging-in-Publication Data
Names: Williamson, Penelope R., author. | Shaw, Darcy H., author.
Title: Writing together : a year of meaning-making and friendship / Penny Williamson and Darcy Shaw.
Description: Includes bibliographical references. | Palisade, CO: Creative Courage Press, 2025.
Identifiers: LCCN: 2025908726| ISBN: 978-1-959921-06-6 (paperback) | 978-1-959921-07-3 (ebook)
Subjects: LCSH Authorship—Collaboration. | Friendship. | Creative writing. | BISAC LANGUAGE ARTS & DISCIPLINES / Writing / Nonfiction (incl. Memoirs) | SELF-HELP / Creativity | FAMILY & RELATIONSHIPS / Friendship
Classification: LCC PN145 .W55 2025 | DDC 808/.02—dc23

Also see Permission Credits in backmatter.

Cover and interior design: KP Books
Editor: Shelly Francis
Proofreader: Rebecca K. Job

Author photo of Penny Williamson: Mike Styer, Mike Styer Photography
Author photo of Darcy Shaw: Michael Needham, UPEI Marketing & Communications

Contents

For Jim, who knew me best and
for Jessie, my heartline.

Penny Williamson

To all those with four legs who helped me
become a better human being.

Darcy Shaw

Introduction

The short story is: We are two friends—Penny and Darcy—who wrote together, weekly, for a year. We had no idea what would emerge, simply wanting to reflect on our lives through writing with a good friend. We invented a process that proved both trustworthy and evocative for each 90-minute session: first reading a poem as a catalyst for reflection and for letting a question emerge as a prompt to write on for 10 to 20 minutes, online; then reading what we wrote to each other, reflecting briefly, and then creating a new question for at-home writing between sessions. We sent our pieces to each other before our next meeting and began our time reading these aloud, and then we went on to a new poem and new writing. After a year, we looked back over our work and found a richness there that we think would be powerful and useful to share.

THE INVITATION

Writing Together is a book for those who have big and small questions, want to write, need a structure, and would like to do it with a friend or friends. It's also for those who are interested to learn how we created a relational space to write together, developed questions (writing prompts), and wrote stories that led us to explore deeper meanings and truths of our lives. You are not alone, and we may serve as company along the way as you create your own stories and discover more of who you are.

OUR STORY

At the start of 2023, we created the process for each writing session and committed to write together weekly for one year, then look back. What emerged in our writing, supported by our process, moved us in a profound way. We spent most of 2024 and into 2025 organizing and writing this book. In it, we share a detailed explanation of our process as well as some of our favorite stories. We've also included some new writing that emerged as we reflected on the experience of writing together and expanded on themes that arose in our stories.

What started out as a writing exercise became an exploration of captivating life questions that we were holding. Questions that drew us into both joyful and dark places, to stories we had never told before (not even to our partners), and to a place where we held each other's vulnerability with the care and respect it deserved. To be fully seen and heard—a rare gift. That is what this book is about and why we wanted to share our process with others.

We are each in a reflective time in our lives and the notion of meaning-making of our accumulated experiences through writing had appeal. Both of us are facilitators who have led many retreats utilizing the Courage & Renewal approach developed by the Center for Courage & Renewal. It was natural to create a process using and expanding on what had served us in our lives, leadership, and retreat work.

We were also influenced by having taken two intensive writing courses online with Natalie Goldberg in 2021 and 2023, which guided our shared writing practice. Natalie's teaching helped normalize the idea that we could actually write and helped us let go of being overly judgmental about our own writing.

Although our friendship seems pretty regular to us, others have commented that it is surprising or unlikely. Stepping back, we can appreciate how it would look that way to some. We are different genders, about 15 years apart in age, and live in different countries. On top of that, we have had very different vocational paths, life experiences, and upbringings. Penny grew up in Manhattan and the suburbs of New York City and was raised by artist parents. Darcy grew up on the prairies of Western Canada; his parents worked in carpentry and nursing, and his grandparents were grain farmers.

Let us introduce ourselves more fully and tell you more about our experience.

ABOUT US

Penny

While in the woods observing and listening to birds as I pursued a doctorate in ecology and animal behavior, it became apparent that the solo life of a field biologist did not speak to my need to be in relation and connected to people and communities. Like the tributaries that feed a river, I explored and developed along many pathways before finding my true home. I apprenticed to skilled therapists to learn empathic listening, asking evocative questions and noticing patterns, and then found my way into medical education as a behavioral scientist. I taught medical students, residents, faculty, and ultimately leaders and their organizations, helping to enhance their skillful means with patients, students, colleagues, and groups. My self-designed approach to learning carried me into formal roles, including associate professor of medicine at Johns Hopkins School of Medicine, leadership positions in several health care organizations, and a successful independent consultancy for over 30 years.

However, I was an outsider, not having formal credentials in the approaches that drew me in. I was often an "only" among groups: the only woman, the only behavioral scientist among physicians, and early on, the youngest person among those I taught. I showed my compassion and respect easily. I hid my professional loneliness behind a mask of humor and projected confidence and competence.

I came to my true home and my true self after I met author/ educator Parker Palmer in 1993 (when I was 50). His teaching made visible to me that I was helping others be what I often did not dare to be—authentic and showing up whole. I had hidden my vulnerability and fears while helping others share themselves and claim their gifts as well as their limits. Parker mentored me and five others as he was developing The Courage to Teach program (later known as the Courage & Renewal approach). I stopped being afraid of who I was not and embraced more wholly who I am.

For almost three decades, I've coached physicians and led retreats for leaders in healthcare and other serving professions in the US, Canada, the UK, and Japan.

I now find myself in a time of meaning-making and, paradoxically, doing that through writing, an activity that was a struggle for me in my professional work for many years.

So much that was unexpected emerged in this year of writing with a friend; I should say writing and reading aloud. Some of it was a kind of loosening of self-judgment and ultimately a giving over to phrases that pleased me and a depth that surprised me. I became less guarded, more honest. I was constantly moved by our synchronicities and by our uniqueness.

We began to recognize our individual styles of writing. Our ways of being in the world showed up in how we described, remembered, and shared our passages. I didn't realize that what I wrote would be moving or interesting to Darcy (or anyone else) and felt similarly, delightfully touched and informed to read how Darcy has experienced his life.

Our appointments with writing became a guidepost every week. I looked forward eagerly to discover where our created topics would take each of us. Often it was like opening a curtain to a remembered story, or series of events that made new sense in the telling. Like that week we read "Sanctuary" by Ada Limón, and I found myself remembering stories about my mother who died young, realizing I knew her better than I thought I did. I found myself able to retrieve details long forgotten and relished hearing/reading the details of Darcy's writing as well, such as what it might be like to live for a day as a goat!

Darcy

I'm a veterinarian and professor emeritus (fancy academic title meaning retired with some lingering university status) in small-animal (dog and cat) internal medicine at the Atlantic Veterinary College, a faculty of the University of Prince Edward Island (PEI) situated on the beautiful Maritime east coast of Canada. Anne of Green Gables country if PEI sounds familiar and you've read the iconic books by Lucy Maud Montgomery. I've spent most of my career here and still teach part time at the veterinary college.

Animals have been an enduring fascination throughout my life. They have, and continue to be, some of my most profound teachers and exemplars. It's no surprise they show up regularly in my writing (and my dreams). My career was largely spent teaching veterinary students and seeing clients with their pets. Administrative roles like department chair and associate dean, as well as being president of the Canadian Veterinary Medical Association, provided opportunities to explore the work of leadership. Over the last twenty years, I've spent considerable time in teaching communication skills and facilitating leadership development within the veterinary profession. That's the snapshot resume story of my career.

The soul story looks different. During the later years of my career, feeling burnt out from clinical work and anxious about impending leadership roles, I sought out personal and professional development programs that would help me adapt. What became apparent was that what I really needed was a chance to reflect on and reconnect with who I was and what deeper purposes drew me forward. I was in my late forties and had experienced my fair share of life's ups and downs. A close friend had died too soon, my father had passed away, and other hoped-for things, like children, had never happened. I had seen a lot of animals suffer and for many, had directly eased their passing through euthanasia. Looking back, I think each one took a small piece of me with them. I lost a sense of myself, felt ungrounded, and was unsure what direction I was headed.

After participating in a leadership development program called Leading Organizations to Health, I joined a retreat series led by Penny and a colleague, called Courage to Lead. In that trustworthy space, I had a chance to reflect and reconnect with who I was and what was important. It was a spiritual journey that I did not know I needed. It was, in many ways, lifesaving. Penny and I became friends during that time.

I followed up the retreat series by completing the facilitator preparation program offered by the Center for Courage & Renewal and was mentored by Penny. Doing the Courage work was transformational for me. Because of this, I felt those in the veterinary profession would welcome an opportunity to do this kind of contemplative work, especially those in leadership roles. As a result, Penny and I offered a number of Courage & Renewal retreats (Leading with Integrity) for veterinarians over the ensuing years. Then COVID happened.

To maintain our connection and continue to explore compelling questions about life, Penny and I started to meet regularly on Zoom. First, it was to talk about interesting books we were reading. After Penny invited me to join her in taking an online writing course from Natalie Goldberg, our meetups evolved into writing sessions that later led us to develop a more disciplined approach.

So how do I feel after that year of writing together? Surprised by what happened and grateful that it did. More settled but more expansive in my thinking about who I am and whose I am. As I age (now in my mid-sixties), I've realized that I hold a lingering anxiety about ossification. That I will become mineralized and fixed in place like bone. Waiting for the creeping loss of flexibility, adaptability, and creativity. My life, like everyone else's, has a lot of loose ends. Ideas, memories, connections left hanging and not tied together in a meaningful way. Writing invited (sometimes pushed) me into engaging with challenging questions that flexed my intellectual, emotional, and spiritual muscles. That has been an unexpected opportunity and gift.

BEGINNING TO WRITE TOGETHER

Setting pen to paper or fingers to keyboard is hard. Where do you start? What do you write about? Good questions that lead to writing prompts are enlivening. They open doors and reveal paths. We used poetry to help develop interesting and compelling prompts. Poems acted as a "third thing" (which we elaborate on in chapter 1), something that we could put in front of us to reflect on to give us writing ideas.

The act of writing revealed surprising insights. It took us farther than we imagined. Simply talking about a question/ prompt never brought us to where writing did. Sharing writing and reading it to someone can be stressful. Questions arise. What can I share? What is safe to share? What will they think of me? What will I think of myself? Creating a welcoming and nonjudgmental space was an important part of our process. So too was committing to each other that we would write regularly for an entire year. What helped was developing a structure that provided a disciplined framework so we could show up, write, share, affirm, and repeat. We met and wrote almost weekly. Neither of us would have done it by ourselves. Being accountable to each other was key.

IN THE PAGES AHEAD

This book has three pieces. First, we provide a detailed description and guidelines for a writing journey that includes finding a friend or friends to write with, committing for a year, and following the same structure for each writing session. Second, we describe elements of the Courage & Renewal approach and how that helped us create an inviting space to write and share in. Finally, we offer our writing prompts, stories that ensued, and our reflections on them and of our experience during this year of writing together.

In chapter 1, we describe why and how our writing process came about. Chapter 2 provides a detailed guide to what each writing session looked like and how you can replicate it. Chapter 3 gives you a behind-the-curtains look at a writing session and the first example of stories we wrote online and at home. Chapters 4 to 13 are filled with compelling writing prompts, selected stories from 11 sessions, and reflections that arose.

We wrote many more stories than we've included in this book. The ones we've shared meant the most to us and range from lighter to more challenging topics. They also show the arc of our deepening friendship over the year as we wrote and shared from an increasingly vulnerable and honest place. Following some closing thoughts in the Epilogue, you'll find Appendix I, where we provide the list of poems and writing prompts used in all our writing sessions. In Appendix II, we share favorite poets and poems that we've also used in past retreats and loved.

You can read *Writing Together* from beginning to end, or just dip your toe into select chapters for examples of writing prompts and stories, or for inspiration. However, we highly recommend reading the detailed guidelines in chapter 2 before setting up your own writing sessions with a friend. Magic can happen in that affirmative space, and it's worth taking the time to create and hold it in a way that will feed and support your shared writing experience.

So, sharpen your pencil, fill up your fountain pen, uncap your marker, or charge your laptop! We invite you to join us for a year of writing, meaning-making, and friendship.

CHAPTER ONE

Origins

From Retreat Work to Writing

I t's time. Time to begin. Time to start thinking about the writing you want to do with a friend and how to do it in a way that invites all of you to show up. To be fully present, poised, and open. We have some ideas about that!

To lay the groundwork, we start with the story behind our writing process by bringing you into the experience of our first shared Courage to Lead retreat, with Penny leading and Darcy participating. This "live account" will introduce you to the seminal practices that we turned to in our year of writing. What shaped us, shaped our process. It all seems so logical in hindsight, and yet we found our way into our writing process intuitively and only later realized that we had adopted these familiar "courage ways" of relating. They were by now our natural handholds.

PENNY

I set my suitcase down on the four-poster bed in what had become "my room" in the lovely old inn where I held my Courage to Lead retreats. Then, as always, I headed out— down the street past the familiar shops, around the corner to catch my first glimpse of the water, and then across the graceful wooden foot bridge that passes over the salt marsh and dunes and onto the beach of Cape Cod Bay. I watched the resident osprey pair soar, and the gulls wing their way in loops over the Bay. I noticed the muted oranges, yellows, and browns of the marsh grasses in this particular October, fall being the time of the first of the five quarterly retreats. Thus began the day of relaxation and inner preparation that I always give myself before the start of a retreat. It is my "work before the work," the time to let go of the busyness of usual work and life in order to bring myself fully to the next three days—to release the myriad anxieties I so often hold about whether my design is good enough, whether I'll be liked by these new participants, whether I'll warm to them, whether they will find the time useful and become a trustworthy community. I had spent many weeks planning the flow and content of the retreat. In giving myself this personal time, I remember once again that my job is to be fully present, welcoming, attentive, and ready, unattached to things that are out of my control. Now, I settled into that knowing.[1]

The next day, I attended to the final details of the retreat ahead, touches that create an environment of beauty and spaciousness: I penned 12 cards of welcome, reflecting on each participant as I wrote their name—some were known to me, others not yet. The innkeepers had set a circle of comfortable chairs in the lovely meeting space, an inviting room with burnished wood floors, a beamed ceiling, and many windows with lace curtains that filtered the light. A low table with a candle, two cups of colored pencils, and some colorful fall leaves was set in the middle of the circle, and several opening quotes and

---

1 For some years I facilitated the Courage to Lead retreats alone. From 2010 onwards, I shared the leadership with my dear friend and colleague, Hanna Sherman. For simplicity, I have written about only my own experience here.

Touchstones[2] were tacked to the walls. Touchstones describe our intentional ways of being together that help create a trustworthy space that is invitational, welcoming, and inclusive. Recalling them for myself as I begin each retreat is another step in my own preparation, as well as a guide for our group. I reviewed the design of the retreat and set out handouts for the first evening, also laying blank journals and pens on each chair. Katherine and Donnie, owners of the inn and now like family after six years, prepared all of our meals, and by evening, the smells of good food added to the hospitable atmosphere. We always started the program with dinner, followed by an introductory session. All was in readiness.

Everyone had arrived by dinnertime except for one participant, Darcy. Travel snafus were always a risk. I texted him to see if he would be there by the start of the evening session and let him know we'd save dinner for him.

***

DARCY

I got Penny's text as I exited US 6 East towards Sandwich. I was about five minutes away, and a wave of exhaustion enveloped me. It had been a long day and a busy week. For most of the week, my veterinary college had been undergoing an accreditation site visit by a team from the Canadian and American Veterinary Medical Associations. Accreditation is on a seven-year cycle and all Canadian and US veterinary colleges and schools participate in this important process. I was associate dean of professional services at the time and had led the year-long preparation for the site visit. I couldn't leave early in the day for Boston as I normally would have because we'd had final exit interviews with the site team all morning.

---

2 The Courage & Renewal Touchstones implicitly shaped our writing sessions. They are described in this chapter, and we include modified Writing Together versions at the end of chapter 2.

I arrived around 6 pm, picked up my rental car, and merged onto I-90 out of Logan International Airport to join the Thursday evening rush hour traffic heading south out of the city. It's about an hour's drive to Sandwich, a town at the base of Cape Cod. This was the first time I'd driven in the Boston area and was anxious about the traffic and missing exits to the route I'd planned. Darkness and intermittent light rain added to the fun!

Pain was settling in behind my eyes and I could feel a migraine creeping in on little hooked feet—something that has dogged (no pun intended) me since I was 10 years old. My body was predictably rebelling against the load I'd been carrying, not only in the last week, but in the last few years. I needed to slow down. I needed to breathe. I was looking forward to the next few days.

I struggled to find the inn's sign in the misting gloom. I had already missed dinner and knew Penny was waiting for me. I leaned over the steering wheel, spied the sign, pulled into the gravel driveway, and parked under a large linden tree. I had arrived. Finally!

Penny greeted me at the door. I shoved my suitcase into a nearby alcove and was shown into the room where 11 other participants were sitting. The group was arranged in a circle with a small table in the center containing a burning candle and some beautiful fall foliage. I eased into a wingback chair, dinner plate in hand, and waited for what was to come.

Everyone was invited to sit in silence for a few minutes. To settle and bring ourselves as fully to the moment as we could. We were then invited to introduce ourselves, or not, in whatever way suited us. After some silence, a participant started. There were a few long periods of quiet in between introductions. Penny never intervened and sat quietly until eventually everyone had spoken. I was surprised that Penny had not gently nudged us along. As an educator who has worked with small groups, I would have had a hard time not prompting people to move along. I usually had a schedule to keep with a limited amount of time to accomplish something. I was impressed. What a generous, respectful, and welcoming way to hold a group. Individual contributions to the group were invitational. As Penny would later mention, this was not a share-or-die event. *Extending welcome* and *being as fully present as we could* with *invitation not demand* were three important Touchstones that guided our interactions.

On that first evening, Penny shared all the Touchstones with our group. I remember thinking they were kind of revolutionary. I had been used to the cut-and-thrust of group interactions in academic life. Not a pleasant experience at times. Here were things that really shifted how I could understand and better my own small- and large-group work. I was curious to see how I would feel being a part of this new dynamic. Other Touchstones like *no fixing or advising; respond with open, honest questions* (more on this later); and *speaking your truth in ways that respect other people's truths* made so much sense given the environment we were trying to create. I saw and felt how powerful they were during this and all other retreats I participated in. The remaining Touchstones guided us to *trust and learn from the silence; observe deep confidentiality;* and *believe that we could emerge refreshed, surprised, and less burdened than when we came.*

Like most people, I found silence in groups challenging. We are so programmed to fill it up with something, whether helpful or not. To think that something good may be happening in that silence was surprising, and after a while, I realized it was unassailably true. Deep confidentiality was for me the last important item needed to create a trustworthy space for our group. What happened, what was said or written, would be held within each of us and within the group. The last Touchstone on emerging refreshed was a big ask in my current bleary state. I had to see it to believe it. Turns out I did!

THE POWER OF OPEN, HONEST QUESTIONS

PENNY

On the second day of the retreat, I introduced the group more fully to the beautiful, countercultural discipline of asking open, honest questions. This practice stems from the Quaker tradition, which believes that each person has their own inner teacher (inner wisdom) to resolve issues and challenges yet needs a trustworthy community to help them uncover their own knowing and discern their way forward. Asking questions is the way in, yet only if the questions are free from judgment or advice. The most powerful questions come from deep and respectful listening to the other person. They are questions only the person being asked could know the answer to. For example, open, honest questions come from the heart rather than the head, such as "What have you experienced in the past that might help you now?" or "If your heart had a voice, what would it say to you?" Open, honest questions are free from the questioner's well-intended "answers disguised as queries," like, "Where might you have learned that?" versus "Don't you think this is because of your mother?" Open, honest questions have 360 degrees of freedom: "How did that make you feel?" versus seeking yes-or-no answers, such as "Weren't you afraid?" or "Weren't you angry or sad?" These generative inquiries open a space for the other person to explore new avenues or deepen their understanding.

In the service of creating a safe learning space as the facilitator and to teach how to ask open, honest questions, I shared a current personal dilemma. I invited the group to practice composing and then asking me their questions and then I commented on whether each question felt like an opening for me to explore, without judgment or advice. At the time of the retreat, I was struggling with an overfull work life with too many commitments and a grueling travel schedule. I was on the point of exhaustion and wanted questions to help me explore how to create more spaciousness in my life so that I could be fully present to the very things that brought me joy and fulfillment.

I asked that someone write down the questions, because I'd want to reflect on them later. A few I remember are: "What are the gifts of your current life?" "What might you miss if you give up some things?" "How have you created space in your life at other times?" "What is your greatest fear?" All were useful questions to contemplate.

This first introduction paved the way for how participants responded to each other in the small-group and large-group interactions that followed. Asking and answering open, honest questions became a repeated practice at the retreat, whether responding to personal stories or reflections upon reading a poem. I was humbled, as always, by each person's willingness to "try on" this counterintuitive practice and witness the impact on themselves as well as the recipients. And I was moved at how participants got the hang of it and asked evocative, open questions from the outset.

I consider this a lifetime discipline, always a practice, as it is all too familiar to fall back into trying to solve others' problems with our own good ideas. Over time, for both Darcy and me, asking open, honest questions became a way of being. We carried it forward into the process we created for our shared writing, as we discuss in the next chapter.

USING THIRD THINGS TO GENERATE QUESTIONS AND WRITING PROMPTS

DARCY

In Courage retreats, poetry and teaching stories are used as "third things." In this context, poems anchor participants' focus and create opportunities to reflect on words, phrases, or questions present in the poem that may speak to their own lives. Understanding the author's intent is not the goal. I think of third things as an indirect or oblique way to sidle up to important life questions without having to stare them directly in the eye. They are a way of easing into the work of self-examination and reflection.

In this first retreat, for example, we read the beautiful poem "Love After Love" by Derek Walcott. The second stanza ends with, "Give back your heart to itself, to the stranger who has loved you all your life, whom you ignored for another." One of Penny's questions for our reflection was, "What would it mean to give back your heart to yourself?" It was our first introduction to this way of working with poetry and how open, honest questions may be used to explore our inner lives.

Before I attended Courage to Lead retreats, I was largely unfamiliar with poetry. Although I've always been a big reader, that did not include poetry. High school exposure to dense and opaque poems that had little obvious relationship to my life put me off the whole genre. I threw the baby out with the bathwater. The selection of inviting poems and how they were used in retreats turned me completely around. Poetry is an exercise in truth-telling and the poems called me to consider what my own truths were. By mid-life I was ready and open for this. As a teenager—well, you can imagine.

Poems are unquenchable question- and insight-generating vehicles. They offer up a rich buffet of unique words, provocative juxtapositions, and compelling phrases that can call forth powerful images and feelings. It's for this reason that we used poems as third things in our writing sessions and created open, honest questions as writing prompts to explore with our pens. In chapter 2, we provide an example of how we did this.

In a broader sense, third things for the purposes of reflection can be many things. An impactful video or song. Visual art or a walk in the woods. In my view, the spirit of third things shows up in many daily activities. Friends gather for an evening of board games or cards. The game is a third thing that creates a space for nonthreatening social interaction which can lead to important conversations. I used to go fishing with my father; I didn't like fishing that much, but he loved it. Fishing was the third thing that gave us a reason to spend some time together and talk about things we may never have talked about in other settings.

PUTTING IT ALL TOGETHER

When we created the process for our year of writing, it happened organically. At the time, we weren't explicitly laying out the Touchstones of the Courage & Renewal approach or deciding how to work with them in shaping our weekly writing sessions. Yet, looking back, we realized that is exactly what happened. The Courage practices and the principles that underlie them had become our way of creating, holding, and being in a trustworthy space.

In this chapter, we have shared core aspects of our first shared retreat to make explicit the origins of our writing process. In the next chapter, we describe our writing process through stories and reflections on a single writing session, to provide guidance for organizing your own writing journey with a friend.

CHAPTER TWO

A Day in Our Writing Process

To give you a more detailed experience of our writing process as well as an example of how we showed up on a certain day, we share the specifics of one writing session that stood out to us as we looked back on the full year. This day happened to be three months into our year of writing together. It was a particularly memorable one we hope will inform as well as inspire you.

By this point, we now looked forward to these writing times with anticipation. After some awkward sessions at the start, often needing to remind ourselves of our process and figure out how best to get ready, we had settled into a comfortable pattern and rhythm. We found a flow that worked. It was so much like the steps before a retreat, except here we were readying ourselves to show up for writing instead of preparing to welcome a group. We were readying ourselves to be fully present, to welcome each other and whatever the writing brought. In retrospect, it feels like we were doing warm-up exercises and gently stretching our writing muscles.

The questions and writing prompts over the first months took us to many places: our beliefs—those that serve and those that don't; the meaning of full hearts; and encounters with strangers that changed us, to name a few. Although we tried to get together every week, travel and other commitments inevitably got in the way. We ended up meeting for 35 writing sessions between January 2023 and February 2024. As previously mentioned, all of the writing prompts and titles of poems used over that period are collected in Appendix I. We also share a list of additional poems that were some of our favorites used in past retreats we've led in Appendix II.

NOTES ON THE PROMPTS AND THE WRITING TOGETHER PROCESS

We created the prompts based on what inspired us from the poems we read, or sometimes, just from how we felt that day. A couple of times we were stymied and sought help (thanks to the reflective questions in Pádraig Ó Tuama's *Poetry Unbound* weekly newsletter on Substack).

Feel free to use our prompts in any way that serves. If you're just starting your writing journey, keep the prompts simple with some specificity (e.g., "Think of a time when a walk in nature amazed you"). Big, nonspecific, and overwhelming existential questions (e.g., "Why does the universe exist?") can stall and frustrate you. Sometimes just a word or a short phrase from a poem can open the way. You can use our prompts as written and see what emerges, or modify them in ways that suit you, or ignore them entirely and create your own. Questions and prompts always have a way of evolving into new and interesting subsequent ones.

During our writing sessions online, we set a timer for 10, 15, or 20 minutes. When beginning, try out 10 minutes to see how that feels. You'll sense when a longer time is right. When the timer went off, we would finish a word or a sentence, then set our pens down. Wherever we stopped was good enough. We always remembered what Natalie Goldberg said in her teaching workshops: during the timed session, keep your pen moving— get out of your judgmental mindset and just write, no editing or worrying about spelling or punctuation, just keep writing.

Also, it reliably brought a smile to our faces recalling her other spoken advice: *You can write the worst shit down. It doesn't matter, it's just practice.*

Think of this chapter as an invitation to be there with us in each of our homes and online. Please don't feel that your first session (or any) should unfold in the same way. Rather, we hope this description may provide guidance for organizing your own writing journey with a friend.

The elements of our writing process are presented here first, at a glance, so that you can recognize how each step appears on a typical day. You can also return to this summary (or agenda, almost) at any time for a reminder. You'll also see some of these phrases in bold below in our narratives to lift up where the practices occurred in our session.

The Writing Together Process

Online (or in person) writing with your partner

- Work before the work: Whatever helps you get ready to write.
- Greetings and settle in silence for a minute or two.
- Consider reading the "Touchstones for Writing Together" aloud to each other.
- Check-in—a few minutes each to update the other(s) about what's going on for you, what's changed since your last meeting, or how you're feeling that day.
- Each person reads their writing from the previous at-home question/prompt.
- Affirm and thank each other.
- Select and explore a third thing (poem, music, etc.).
  - Notice words, phrases, images, feelings—what open, honest questions arise?

- Create a writing prompt, question, or topic and agree on writing time (10, 15, or 20 minutes).
- Settle in silence for a few minutes, then begin your timed writing.
- When the time is up, read your writing to each other and offer affirmations and thank yous.
- Come back to the third thing and/or images or thoughts that came up in your timed writing.
  - What further questions arise?
  - Discuss what emerges and settle on a question/ prompt for at-home writing.
- Schedule your next meeting time.

At-home writing

- Consider what's needed to help you sit down and write.
  - Character of the space (quiet, out of the way, good light)
    - What time of day works best for you?
  - How do you like to write (computer, pen and paper)?
    - If it's pen and paper, is it the right pen, the right paper?
  - How much time do you need to set aside (30 minutes, an hour)?
  - What mood is most conducive? If you're busy and overwhelmed on your chosen writing day, maybe do it another day.
- Bottom line: don't worry. Just write.

A WRITING DAY

PENNY

Today was my favorite way to start a day—sitting in meditation for 20 minutes, then a shower and quick breakfast and out for a walk on the Schuylkill River Trail on this sunny spring morning, already 60 degrees by 6 am with a projected high of 79 degrees Fahrenheit. This was my "work before the work" for today and for each writing session. By the time of our meeting, I was in a relaxed, expectant mode—ready to see what the day's writing would bring, having learned that I never could tell in advance.

As always, I was happy to see Darcy appear on Zoom—the still-magical arrival of a friend with the click of a link. We set each meeting for 90 minutes so that we never had to feel rushed and could give each part of our process the time it needed, creating a climate of spacious welcome. We started as always with a **few minutes of silence** to let ourselves settle and then had a **check-in**—time to share what had occurred in our lives since our last meeting: our state of mind, whatever was "up" for us. I was excited by the full onset of spring, seeing it with fresh eyes in my new city of Philadelphia. I told Darcy about some lovely walks and the particular specialness of being with my new partner in this season of beginnings, and marveled at hearing his stories of biking in the much colder Prince Edward Island, spring being farther behind that far north. Then **we read aloud to each other what we had written at home from our previous session.**

This preamble to our day's writing was, as always, marked by welcome and affirmation, and the familiarity of being with a good friend in a known process.

DARCY

I make my way up the stairs carefully, overly full coffee cup in hand, trying not to drip any along the way. I don't drink a lot of coffee, but I like at least one good cup per day. By "good"

I mean strong and full, the kind of coffee that announces itself and fills your senses with chocolate roasted notes and thoughts of the exotic places it came from. My cup is small, a slightly cracked, green-lipped, white relic from a 1960s-style diner. I love its unpretentiousness and the stories it could tell of the countless times someone brought it to their lips. Were they thinking of how good or bad, hot or cold the coffee was, or were they wrapped up in their to-do lists, worries, or what news the friend sitting across from them was sharing?

It's a typical April day in the Canadian Maritimes. If you've spent time in this region, you know cold, wet days predominate at this time of year. Most people here try to get away to warmer climes around now, even though the snow is mostly gone and temperatures are rising. The reason is that this goes on for what seems like forever. The nice, warm summer weather that graces Prince Edward Island often does not settle in until mid-June. Ugh!

I got more wet than usual this morning because I went for a swim at a local pool. A faint smell of chlorine still lingers as I sit down in my small office and open the laptop. I set the coffee on my desk, proud that I have not spilled any. Small victories to celebrate! My body feels deeply relaxed and liquid after the swim. There is something about swimming that gives me a post-exercise buzz more than any other vigorous activity. I wonder if it has something to do with buoyancy and being held and caressed as you move through the water.

Penny appears on my screen. I do too, of course, and make a mental note to shave closer to our next call. I inherited vigorous facial hair growth from my father, as well as its alter ego, early onset pattern baldness. I was always struck with that paradox. Hair everywhere else on my face, just not on the top of my head. It didn't get the "grow hair" memo, I guess. Since I don't work full time anymore, I have become more relaxed about shaving. A good close shave with a razor will last two days, kind of. By the third day, I'm looking decidedly hirsute and would be looked at questionably in a dark alley. Thankfully, Penny is generous enough to overlook my grooming shortcomings.

I look forward to our check-in. It is spring after all, and the birds are starting to return. Grackles showed up this week and started devouring the contents of our feeder in their headlong rush into breeding season. I so love how birdsong reappears after a long, quiet winter. That signals spring to me more than anything else. I tell Penny about this in our check-in. Since she studied ornithology, I know she will appreciate it. I try to get her to identify the bird behind a birdsong. You know, the one that has two tones and goes from a high to low note like "eee dee." I try to whistle this, but most of my effort ends up on my computer screen. Good thing I have some tissues nearby.

We read last week's at-home writing to each other. It was about what compels us to go miles and miles to know better. I love hearing Penny talk about how what compels her now at 80 has shifted from working with organizations to "being with" people one on one. Being more truly with herself and still passionately interested in what's next. She finishes up with, "This is not the time to hide behind old habits. I am an imperfect, loving, sometimes fully present human, and that is a good thing. Sometimes it is even good enough. Never let it be said that I am a sloth in the face of all that life has given me. Never." Words to live by.

I read my response to the at-home writing prompt and describe how I was compelled by my enduring curiosity about pretty much anything and everything, especially when it comes to nature and animals. I used painting and filling in blank spaces as a metaphor for my compulsion and ended with, "This is a picture I need to paint. It's never quite finished but boy, am I curious to know what it will look like when I put the last dab of paint on or add the last brushstroke. With my last breath, I hope to see it shimmering in front of me so I can fall in love, for the last time, with all that was."

Turning to Our Next Poem

Although both of us have large collections of favorite poems, we chose to instead use Pàdraig Ó Tuama's book *Poetry Unbound:*

50 *Poems to Open Your World.*[3] Every week we'd turn to a new poem, never knowing what to expect. It exposed us to an abundance of new authors and topics. This also prevented us from relying on the familiar poems we loved while challenging ourselves to see the world from different perspectives. If after two readings a poem didn't speak to us, we gave ourselves permission to turn to the next one. In this way, the book provided our source of third things, but we were not bound by its chronology. As we rolled the poems around in our minds, we asked open, honest questions to each other, often going back and forth to wordsmith a question until it captured something that drew us in to write about.

The next poem in Pádraig Ó Tuama's book was "A Blessing" by James Wright. **We each read the poem aloud, letting the words and images land in us,** having experienced how fruitful it is to read a poem aloud and also to hear it read in another voice. In chapter 3, we will share the poem, process, and resulting writing from this day in more detail. For the purposes of this chapter, where we describe a typical writing session, we will skip ahead. As always, **we used the poem as a third thing—something to place between us, reflecting on what words or phrases touched us**, what spoke to our hearts, rather than interpreting what the author might have meant.

Out of our reflections and our earlier check-in, **we created a prompt for our online writing**. As we talked more about the physical sensations evoked by the poem, we were drawn to address in greater detail how the body feels the things it does. A prompt like "Describe your sensual memories of a recent time" suited our purposes. We are both very curious about the wisdom that lives within our bodies and how that informs how we show up to ourselves and the world (a topic we explore further in chapter 5).

---

3 Pàdraig Ó Tuama, *Poetry Unbound: 50 Poems to Open Your World*, W. W. Norton & Company, 2023.

Once we had our prompt, **we sat in silence for three minutes, then wrote for an agreed-upon time** of 15 minutes. Each of us muted our sound and began to write.

PENNY

I never know in advance what will emerge when I put pen to paper. Today I am ready with all the sensual recollections of my recent river walks. The sights, sounds, smells, and feelings of being fully present flow onto the page. They are right there, waiting to be tapped. Who knew? I am surprised at the specificity of my recall.

We stop at the end of online writing time, taking a few seconds to finish a sentence. Then **each of us reads aloud** what we have written. Natalie Goldberg taught us that reading aloud and being witnessed without judgment is an essential part of writing practice. It helps you hear your voice differently, less critically, and to know what your mind is holding. I am touched again to **experience being witnessed and listened to with affirmation and acceptance** by Darcy. He thanks me and reads his piece. As I listen, I can feel each sensation of Darcy's recent swim in an indoor pool. This is fun. I'm happy we can recall our senses in this explicit way.

Darcy agreed it was no surprise that our online writing topic related to sensual memories, given the physicality of "A Blessing." Also, it was not unexpected that he turned to explore what his body was feeling during his recent swim that morning.

Deciding on an At-Home Writing Prompt

We reflect a little on how being specific with sounds, smells, sights, and kinesthetic memories makes writing more interesting, more alive. Then **we consider what we want to explore for our at-home writing.** We return to the haunting lines in the poem: "They love each other. There is no loneliness like theirs." A spark of memory stirs about how opposite emotions can coexist in unlikely ways.

We play with variations and then find our prompt for at-home writing: "When have you held love and loneliness together?" Our hearts drop a little as we sense the depth of this prompt. We can tell it's a courageous one that will take us to a vulnerable place. We feel its tension, its pull, and are willing to try. This is the kind of open, honest question we have taught and practiced in our retreats. It takes us both a bit by surprise, sensing we have ventured into deeper waters than before. **We agree it is a question we wish to explore for our at-home writing.**

PENNY

I did not know until I wrote on this question later in the week that I would put words to paper for the first time about feelings I had not admitted before, even to myself. I had found a place of safety within myself to write about very private memories. It is a testament to our friendship and the trust and safety of our intentional writing space that I also felt able to read what I wrote to Darcy at our next session. Here I was full of spring and new love. Unexpectedly that very delight opened me to the shadow side of love—to the loneliness I had experienced along with love in my marriage of 31 years.

We did not always write about profound or difficult topics, but we noticed that as the year progressed, we were more comfortable going there when called. Stories that had never been told to others arose. We didn't hold back. Humor and laughter came out as well as sadness and tears. Had we not created and maintained a trustworthy space guided by the Touchstones, I don't think this would have happened. Our best selves and our best writing showed up and was welcomed.

Of course, we sometimes came to our writing sessions having had less than a perfect morning, life being life. Sometimes we were rushed, sleep deprived, out of sorts, whatever . . . no matter what, we were always committed to writing during our sessions. We never gave ourselves a pass. We believed that the practice and discipline of writing were paramount. Even on down days, we wrote and we listened to each other with affirmation and non-judgment. Nor did we censor ourselves as we wrote. It mattered.

GUIDELINES FOR CREATING SAFE SPACE

It was only on looking back that we realized we were "living" the Touchstones. We didn't begin each session by formally reciting these guideposts (although that may be helpful as you begin to get comfortable with the process) for how we wanted to be together. Yet they informed the shape and texture of our sessions. In writing about our process, we hope to share what it looked and felt like to manifest these long-held practices. You don't need to have experienced a retreat to set up a trustworthy writing experience. It is a matter of being intentional about how you structure your writing time with a friend, which we pass along as a predictable way to bring out the best in each of you. For it is only when we feel safe within ourselves and with another that we can write freely what is inside. By sharing explicitly how we modified the Courage & Renewal Touchstones and how they informed all aspects of our Writing Together sessions, we demonstrate how you can use them in your own shared writing journeys.

Touchstones for Writing Together[4]

Be as fully present as possible

Give and receive welcome

Trust and learn from the silence

When the going gets rough, turn to wonder

Listen deeply and with generosity

---

4 Adapted from the Touchstones from the Center for Courage & Renewal. https://couragerenewal.org/courage-renewal-approach/

Respond to each other with open, honest questions and affirmations

No fixing, no advising, no correcting each other

Observe robust confidentiality

Know that it's possible to leave the session with whatever it is you need, and that what is discussed, read, or written will continue to grow and evolve

In summary, consider the Touchstones for yourself:

Think about how you can show up 100 percent to be fully present. For Penny it was through meditation and a morning walk; for Darcy, an early morning swim and attention to every aspect of a treasured cup of coffee.

How do you give and receive welcome? We showed with our smiles and greetings that we were happy to see each other on Zoom and were attentive in hearing each other's check-ins as we began.

How do you make room for silence? We built silence into our 90 minutes, both formally (a couple of minutes of silence before we began) and in the spacious pacing of our time. We each muted our sound when we wrote online, to block the noise of scratching pens or background noise.

How does turning to wonder enter into your process? We listened to each other with quiet, focused attention, without interruption. We listened from our hearts, receptive to the many times when tender, unique, humorous, or uncomfortable thoughts were expressed. We were open to our differences as well as to the experiences that resonated between us.

How can you listen deeply to each other with full presence and not give advice, critique, or corrections? We simply offered appreciation for the courage to share and the honor to be invited in. Because many writing groups are all about feedback and critique, this Touchstone may feel especially countercultural. Try sharing your writing without "editing feedback" to see how it feels to simply be witnessed.

What role do open, honest questions play? We created our own open, honest questions and invited ourselves into explorations in writing, never demanding results from ourselves or the other, receptive to discovery.

Whatever is shared is confidential, not to be passed along to others. This more traditional Touchstone is the *sine qua non* of creating a trustworthy space.

What needs are addressed by your writing time together? How might that evolve and impact future sessions? We had come to anticipate the fruitfulness of our writing sessions and routinely ended the 90 minutes feeling more refreshed, surprised, and less burdened than when we began.

What would happen in our writing sessions was unknown, but **we had faith that whatever the outcome, it would serve us in some positive way**. Time and again this came true. Even on days when our writing felt uninspiring, the time spent together lifted our spirits. We stayed curious about the next new writing prompt for the coming week. We just never knew where it would take us.

You will find your own ways of practicing these life-giving Touchstones. We invite you to begin.

CHAPTER THREE

Crossing a Threshold

In chapter 2 we took you through a specific day in our writing process as a guide for your own practice. In this chapter, we return to the same day and the same poem, sharing in depth how our check-in and reflections on the poem "A Blessing" led us to our writing prompt and the stories that emerged when we wrote online. We also share our responses to what we wrote and heard in our readings, and how this led to the creation of a new prompt and our resulting "at-home" writing. We end with our musings on what we wrote at home and elaborate on two pivotal themes that recur throughout this book: the importance of paradox and the transformative power of creating a sanctuary for truth-telling.

As we've explored already, any poem you choose serves as a "third thing"—something to place in the space between you for reflection. As you listen to the other person read it aloud, you might notice what stands out to you. Then take turns sharing words or phrases that touch you, that speak to your hearts, rather than interpreting what the author might have meant. Sparked by these reflections, it is a natural next step to craft a question for your own writing.

A few poems we used are reprinted in full because they were especially moving or generative. For those not included, they are easy to find online or in Pàdraig Ó Tuama's book *Poetry Unbound: 50 Poems to Open Your World.*

A BLESSING

Just off the highway to Rochester, Minnesota
Twilight bounds softly forth on the grass.
And the eyes of those two Indian ponies
Darken with kindness.
They have come gladly out of the willows
To welcome my friend and me.
We step over the barbed wire into the pasture
Where they have been grazing all day, alone.
They ripple tensely, they can hardly contain their
    happiness
That we have come.
They bow shyly as wet swans. They love each other.
There is no loneliness like theirs.
At home once more,
They begin munching the young tufts of spring in the
    darkness.
I would like to hold the slenderer one in my arms,
For she has walked over to me,
And nuzzled my left hand.
She is black and white,
Her mane falls wild on her forehead,
And the light breeze moves me to caress her long ear
That is delicate as the skin over a girl's wrist.
Suddenly I realize
That if I stepped out of my body I would break
Into blossom.

James Wright

This writing session took place in late April. It was early springtime and each of our check-ins (see chapter 2) reflected our delight at being active and out in nature. This was a perfect lead-in to reading the poem, so full of embodied, tactile language. We were moved by the descriptive and sensory images, so immediate we could have been there. We lifted up particular words: "ripple tensely," "can hardly contain their happiness," "they love each other," "there is no loneliness like theirs." The physicality and evoked sensations of "A Blessing" filled us. We were swept up in a sensory whirlwind that we knew to be true, a wholeness that was reflected back to us by the presence of the two ponies—a wholeness that resides in all animals, and which for Darcy has been a lifelong anchor and salvation. Words like "bow shyly," "nuzzled my left hand," and "caress her long ear" led us to our online writing question. It directly addressed what we were reading, feeling, and imagining. It landed on the fertile ground of our experiences of the previous days.

(Note that in the online writing we share, we've made minor edits to correct spelling and grammar. But remember, it's not about writing perfect prose!)

PENNY ONLINE
Describe your sensual memories of a recent time.

Last week, on a stunningly warm and beautiful day, I went for a walk that turned into a journey! I intended to walk for an hour or so, but the beauty and delights around me compelled me on and on and I ended up walking for four hours—nine miles in total.

It was a feast for the senses. Just a few days before, the leaves and flowers were beginning to sprout. On this day everything had burst into extravagant bloom. The soft pink drooping boughs of the weeping cherries lined part of the Schuylkill River trail. That color almost makes me weep, it is so lovely and delicate. A little way further, the clumps of white blossoms on another kind of cherry tree had me laughing at their robust beauty—like the older sister of the first.

I walked onto the grass from the paved path and felt the softness and green-ness even beneath my sneakers. Then there was a cleared dirt section with some mud through which I carefully picked my way, aware of the change in texture.

The river was choc-a-bloc full with rowing teams—sculls with muscled young men and athletic, fit women gliding past in exact formation, being guided by the coxswain with their shouts of "Stroke! Stroke! Stroke!"

The air (having been cold and rainy the day before) was blissfully warm and gentle with breezes that carried trace scents of blossoms, of grass, of spring awakening. I felt my feet and legs strong and stretching as I walked, loving the physicality of striding along, taking in the city, being in full bloom myself.

After a few hours I felt hungry and was lucky enough to find a cafe. They had limited fare. I bought a Danish pastry (something I never do) and sat on a rough stone wall back on the river, relishing the sticky sweet caramel and chewy dough of this forbidden food.

I often hum under my breath and sometimes I listen to music when I walk. I was doing both—and at one point felt such alive joy I began to dance as I walked, moving to the beat of the music, not caring how I looked (as if that would have mattered to anyone)!

On days like this I smile a lot.

DARCY ONLINE
Describe your sensual memories of a recent time.

It's been six weeks since my last time. I've missed it. I step briefly into the lukewarm shower and then walk along the narrow 30-foot hallway, water dripping and feeling chilled. It's good because I know it will feel warmer once I'm in. As I enter the pool area, the warm air and smell of chlorine envelops me. A good smell. Good memories here. I put my towel on a shelf and carefully tread across the pool deck to the far side where the swim lanes are. I gaze anxiously, hoping to have a lane to myself. Thankfully there are two open. I stop by the edge of the farthest lane, don my swim goggles, and climb down the ladder.

Coolness embraces me and I let my whole body slip beneath the surface. I rise up, push off, and begin my front crawl. I so love the clarity of the water and the sharpness of the painted swim lane lines on the bottom of the pool. Nothing like a good set of goggles. The first length is always relaxed as I'm not fatigued yet. I glide through the water without taking a breath until I'm halfway to the other side. Bubbles gradually escape my nose as I empty my lungs. I then turn my head to the left and take a deep breath just as my left arm rises out of the water behind me. Down I go again. Bubbles flowing down my face and chest, muscles in my shoulders tighten side to side as I take deep scoops. I must remember to kick my legs. I often forget this important propulsion system as I focus on my breathing and arms. Glide, breathe, glide, the dance of the water and me.

FINDING THE RIGHT PROMPT

We read our stories to each other and let the impact of the words settle. We are delighted with our recall of specific embodied sensations, sparked by the poem. Now, as in each session, we reflect on what question we might be moved to create for our at-home writing—the piece each of us will write before our next online session. We return to the poem for inspiration and this time (as noted in chapter 2), we are drawn to the haunting lines: "They love each other. There is no loneliness like theirs."

After several iterations, the question comes to us: "When have you held love and loneliness together?" An interesting thing happens when we hit on the right prompt. We both know it. It lands somewhere just below our thinking minds, an internal knowing. We agree instantly that this is what we will write about during the week, to read to each other when we next meet online, as always, after a check-in. We will also send a copy of what we write to each other in advance.

We set a date for our next session, wish each other a good week, and sign off. Our solo writing awaits.

PENNY
What Makes "Unsayable Truths" Sayable?

When we created the prompt, "When have you held love and loneliness together?" I felt myself gasp a little. Something in me stirred—a kind of anticipatory opening—and I sensed I would access what was waiting to be written, even though I wasn't sure what that would be. I remember thinking, "Oh. We are going to write about stuff at a deeper level."

I pick up my pen and begin to write a truth I've hardly admitted, even to myself. Now the words come and I let them come. I write what has been hidden inside me. It feels real, painful, sad, beautiful, and relieving to put these words on paper. I can bear to say them now. I have crossed some threshold inside me. I worry briefly about reading what I'm writing to Darcy, but it doesn't stop me. I trust Darcy. And anyway, I'm not really writing for Darcy. I'm writing for myself. It comes to me that I am just a human person with my own stories. We all have stories. Mine are not so precious. They don't need to be locked away or kept in the dark places in my soul.

After so many years of being nearly paralyzed from writing "unsayable truths," it has taken only three months of writing together to get to this place of safety. What made this possible? I had been so reluctant for so long to write about my life—particularly those experiences, relationships, and feelings that felt too private, unacceptable, embarrassing, dangerous to talk about. That changed during my year of writing with Darcy. I am trying to make sense of what happened because I think it could predictably happen for others as well.

Partly it was our structure. Darcy and I developed an interesting and reliable structure for our writing and made the commitment to write every week for a year. We became comfortable with our process, a known road map for the mysteries that would unfold. We had a firm commitment. Even when

I didn't feel like writing, I knew I would honor that commitment to Darcy and so I wrote anyway.

Along with structure, I want to name our deepening friendship. We built an ever-more-robust trust with each other and experienced increasing ease with writing, sharing, and reading aloud what we wrote. This was due in large part to our affirmative, nonjudgmental way of being together. We accepted each other's words without critique, a welcoming stance that was constant and life-giving. (Thanks to Natalie Goldberg's wise guidance and our "no fixing" touchstone, we offered neither praise nor correction—simply being a supportive witness for each other.)

I read each selection to Darcy and he didn't run away! Far from it. He was appreciative, open, accepting. He didn't judge me. He simply listened. I did the same for him. We were in it together, giving each other affirmation and courage. I began to reframe my life experiences as "just a human story" that I could write and tell to a trusted friend without need to safeguard my feelings. I even thought it would be okay if others read what I wrote. As we shared our weekly offerings, we came to know each other in a fuller way than we had before. We were already good friends; our writing took our friendship to a new level. A friendship of truth-telling was at the center of the power of this year.

We explored a range of topics, experimenting with sharing feelings and stories from our lives, covering grand sweeps of time as well as small moments. We got better at sensing which questions would unearth the richest veins and honed our ability to ask them (drawing on our years of practice in asking open, honest questions as Courage facilitators). I got more comfortable with writing and reading aloud to Darcy and looked forward to hearing what he wrote. What had felt early on like a bit of a chore became a high point in my week. I actually anticipated my writing times with pleasure. I sensed the same might be true for Darcy. We were on a parallel journey and this mutuality was key in keeping me in the game.

Slowly I experienced a shift, an inner easing and permission-giving to write about whatever came up without censoring myself. At first I only hinted at harder topics. Slowly it became possible to go further. In writing, I admitted things to myself I'd never said aloud. This may seem easy from the outside, but I knew I'd crossed a Rubicon.

I began to let go of my long-held worry that my honest sharing could hurt others, cause me to be hurt, or be thought less of. Perhaps I had feared my own self-judgment most of all. My experiences became more acceptable to myself. I began to see that writing weekly for a year could be a way to make meaning of my life.

This day was the day I realized that I had stepped across a river that had seemed fierce and wide, uncrossable. I was ready. Here is what I wrote at my little desk with my view of the river and cityscape beyond, and then read to Darcy—without trepidation—at our next session:

PENNY AT-HOME
When have you held love and loneliness together?

It is hard to admit—at least it was hard to admit to myself during many years—that I was lonely many times being married to Jim. It feels disloyal now that he's gone, and also because we came to love each other for who we were. Yet that very accommodation to our natures carried with it a well of loneliness. Jim didn't find it natural or even possible to talk about feelings. We had fabulous talks about ideas and experiences, and laughter and walks and meals, and (oddly, I always felt) he knew me better than anyone. But it was an intuitive knowing, not a knowing through conversation. It wasn't through words, and words are my way in.

I loved and thought it funny that Jim, who was a marvelous writer, always bought me birthday or anniversary or Valentine's cards that had extravagant printed messages, romantic to the hilt. I'm talking about more than romance here. I longed for something unnamable—more together time and sharing emotions, struggles, feelings, hopes, fears. We couldn't really talk easily about conflicts (I might attempt to start, but you need two people). I'm glad we didn't have many conflicts.

Jim loved me as best he could. I knew that and let go of wishing for something different. I felt at times he didn't think about what I might want or need and so we lived parallel lives in a way. We came to plan our weeks without consulting each other, except for most Sundays and carefully orchestrated vacations once a year. Those times were my favorites. We spent such lovely hours together then—still without soulful talking, but satisfying and close.

When Jim was sick, for the last six months, his heart opened more and he felt more accessible, more expressive. We never talked about his dying. I asked him only once if he was angry about his illness (I blurted it out, having learned over 30 years how loath he was to go to dark places). He got angry then, saying, "Why would I be angry?" It was the end of that conversation. We couldn't talk about other more intimate things ever—he just wouldn't.

I loved him dearly and he knew me better than anyone and loved me dearly as well.

And I was often lonely.

DARCY
Rendering a Regret

When I stared at the stark, incisive simplicity of "When have you held love and loneliness together," I realized the real work was just beginning. What I thought was deep exploration was in reality, the shallow end of a large pool. The actual bottom is not visible and likely never will be. The love and loneliness question was asking for the truth, my truth, unvarnished, unspoken, and as yet unwritten. I'll know it's the truth because there will be an ache in my heart and tears in my eyes. My body knows, it always does. Hard truths live there, whispering gently, patiently waiting to be drawn upward from the unfathomable. Can I do this despite myself?

My mind is more interested in protecting an imaginary stoic or heroic self and the aspirational origin story that goes with it. A story that like the early morning mist, rapidly dissipates once the rising sun's light shines through.

I pick up my fountain pen (a talisman and tool that settles me for the work), close my eyes, and think, *love and loneliness, where are you?* I let the words settle and sink in. Ah, there it is, a melancholy twinge in my chest tugs me into murky waters. It's like the undertow of a rip current that you can't swim against. Tendrils of time and regret encircle and drag me under. I see it resting gently in the weeds—no children. I have love in my life and yet, the blank space in my story line for the name of a child remains unfilled and always will be. And it hurts. There's my loneliness. Pen touches page. It's time to tell the truth, the whole truth.

DARCY AT-HOME
When have you held love and loneliness together?

Ellie (short for Eleanor) was pushing a perambulator along the sidewalk on a sunny, cool winter afternoon in January. There was a lull in the snow and bitter cold. After a few days of warm weather, sidewalks and streets had become bare except for the gravel and litter that melting snow inevitably leaves. We were having a conversation, or more accurately, Ellie was doing the lion's share of the talking while I was trying to listen closely and translate the meaning into an adult context.

You see, Ellie was 6 years old, and I was 58. A significant gap when it comes to priorities in one's life and how you communicate them. The perambulator contained a treasured doll and was a vintage child's version probably built in the '50s. It had large rubber-clad spoked wheels with a metal frame and spring suspension. The beige basket was vinyl-clad with a retractable hood to protect the precious contents from sun and rain.

I was in town for a short visit to do some teaching at the University of Calgary veterinary school. Ellie and her younger brother Gus, my grandniece and nephew, were staying with my sister for a couple of days. Suffice it to say, my sister Debbie recognized this as an opportunity for Ellie to spend some quality time with her great uncle.

Ellie was bundled up, perambulator readied, and we were hustled out the door. It was a lovely walk. We did a circle around the neighborhood. At the last corner, a woman in an SUV turned into the street in front of us and looked our way. A large smile filled her face when she saw us. I suspect she was thinking "Aw isn't that cute. A little girl with her baby carriage out for a walk with . . ." whoever she thought I was (father, grandfather . . .).

So what does this have to do with love and loneliness? The magical little moment I had with Ellie on that brisk winter day brought both of those major-league emotions into sharp focus. Why? Because I always wanted a little girl to raise, and it never happened. I have been fortunate to love and be loved by people like my wife, Shelley, and my sister. I'm hugely grateful for that. At the same time, there is a special lonely space in my heart that will never be filled. The love for and by a child is something I longed for and something I never understood until after it was too late.

So why didn't it happen? Multiple reasons. All seemed reasonable at the time. Less so now. Shelley and I were in our mid-thirties before we felt ready. Our careers were established, and we had good-paying and stable jobs. However, infertility stymied us. Not unexpected at our ages. We tried some treatments but did not get aggressive. It was having a negative impact on our relationship. In the end, I chose Shelley and let the idea of a child go. Neither of us had the energy for alternatives like adoption. We just let it all slowly settle beneath the waves with barely a ripple. No ceremony, no grieving, no looking back—at least initially.

There is a loneliness that comes from not knowing a different kind of love. Having another person in your life that knows all of you, your beauty and your scars. I still get twinges when I see little girls in the grocery store with their parents.

Prancing down the aisles, prattling on about whatever is occurring in the moment. I so wanted to be involved in that chatter, to spoil them with cool clothes, and do goofy things to make them laugh. I'm mindful of how I have built this up. The mirage of heavenly child-rearing. I'm conveniently overlooking the exhaustion and sleepless nights newborns bring and the potentially tumultuous adolescent and teenage years. When the glow of little-girl adoration for their parents can turn into boredom or at worst, disdain. Regardless, my rose-colored glasses are still firmly perched on my nose.

I've largely made peace with all of this. I still get occasional stabs in my heart, but the gyrations of emotion are less. I'm more mindful and grateful for the love that I do have in my life and do my best to honor and be fully present to that. Life moves forwards not backwards. Who knows what might have been. Not having children allowed me to do many things that have been pivotal in shaping who I currently am. I've impacted others' lives in ways that likely would not have happened. I still wonder though, but not too much. I don't want to get lost in the what-if labyrinth. Life is too short. I want to honor all that I did (and will do) and all that I did not. To live fully and love what is in front of me, moment by moment. It's enough. It's enough.

A SANCTUARY FOR TRUTH-TELLING & PARADOX

DARCY

As always, reading our at-home writing is where we began our next session. After hearing Penny read her response, I am without words. The gravity and courage of her writing pierces me. She told the truth, beautiful and hard. If there was any doubt in my mind that we have entered a new place in our writing and friendship, none remains now. I am lifted and settle in to reading my story to Penny, hoping that I will not choke up during the telling. She receives it with an open heart, seeing another part of who I am. Until you begin to understand the pain another person is carrying, can you know them at all? I sense we are both a bit overwhelmed at what just happened. I feel a new energy about our writing. The space we created to support our writing may have become a special garden of truth-telling. To write and read out loud our own ignored, precious, and difficult truths into being, brought us into a more fulsome understanding of what it is to be human and to be a friend.

DARCY
The Universality of Paradox

Penny and I talk about the paradox captured by love and loneliness. We are both familiar with this mind-stretching concept of opposite facts that can both be true. During retreats we often included a session on paradox, recognizing that our lives are full of them when we take the time to look. Nature provides a host of examples. Plants need light and dark. Death, and sometimes destruction, must occur for new life to begin (regrowth after forest fires). Animals, including us, need to be active and need to rest. The cycle of nature shows us the way of paradox. Lush and exuberant life bursts forth in the spring and summer because of death and dormancy in the fall and winter. Each season has its own passing and poignant beauty. Paradox lives in our human capacities.

How is it that vulnerability can be a source of strength, not weakness? Paradox can be a powerful teacher. I smile when I think of what F. Scott Fitzgerald said related to paradox. "The test of a first-rate intelligence is the ability to hold two opposing ideas in mind at the same time and still retain the ability to function." Recognizing paradox and doing my best to hold it with some degree of understanding has allowed me to see the world as it really is, not how I wish it to be. Surprisingly, it has calmed me down and left me more open. Paradox holds profound wisdom and it's no surprise it shows up in the teachings of many wisdom traditions and religions.

One of the hardest paradoxes I held as a veterinarian was preserving life and promoting death, often in the same animal.

I worked hard to preserve life and ease suffering in my dog and cat patients (I took an oath for that), and I also eased their deaths through euthanasia. Another paradox was that I held this preserve life/promote death paradox better earlier in my career versus later. One would think you would get used to it over time but for me, it got more difficult. By the time I retired from clinical practice, I had seen too many animals die. It was harder and harder to be the one who ended lives, no matter how good the reason. You never solve a paradox, but with time and patience, and sometimes love, forgiveness, and compassion, you find a way to hold it and be at peace with that part of you and that part of the world.

PENNY
Paradox in Plain Sight

I have come to feel the ironic truth that life's paradoxes always point out the beauty of what "is" set against the agony or longing for what "isn't." The opportunity and challenge is to hold both while choosing what is life-giving in every moment.

When I began to write of these more private and unspoken feelings, I did so not knowing if Darcy would do the same. Perhaps I would be alone in sharing this unspoken pain. I did it anyway, knowing it was the right time for me. It was especially poignant, therefore, to be "met" with Darcy's courageous writing. We had metaphorically stepped together through this opening into a new level of sharing. (Let me add that we weren't always in sync. Sometimes only one of us might go deep in response to a writing prompt. It was an unspoken, vital condition of our writing that we only wrote our truths, no more, no less. We had created a trustworthy container for us to support and affirm whatever emerged.)

When Darcy read aloud what he had written, I was moved to tears. I felt the ache of his words and the honor of hearing them. To witness such depth of feeling was a gift. Today we trusted ourselves and each other enough to travel into fragile terrain, places we had not ventured, and write the long-hidden words of our feelings. I felt a lightening. I wasn't alone in writing about a complicated truth. Nor was Darcy alone in putting his experience into words.

The paradox in plain sight was that writing with a friend about loneliness and love made it more bearable. Perhaps we gave each other the courage to let our feelings see the light of day. I sensed that new depths would open as we continued our weekly writing. It was a remarkable moment.

> We shake with joy, we shake with grief.
> What a time they have, these two
> housed as they are in the same body.
>
> **Mary Oliver**

CHAPTER FOUR

Layers of Truth

I n this and the chapters ahead are a selection of our favorite stories (online and at-home) rather than everything we wrote over the year. In our eyes, these particular stories were more interesting, stretched us in some way, or spoke to themes we were drawn to. We hope you enjoy them.

We now take you with us during one week of writing. Sparked by Zaffar Kunial's evocative poem "The Word," we began with a lighthearted topic for our online writing. The release of humor and giving ourselves permission to follow our hearts opened the way for a deeper dive with a compelling prompt for our at-home writing. This in turn led to further reflective pieces that took each of us into unexpected territory—unearthing and exploring old memories, venturing into more courageous sharing and truth-telling, discovering new layers of clarity and unspoken truths, and making new meaning from what we found.

THE WORD

I couldn't tell you now what possessed me
to shut summer out and stay in my room.

Or at least attempt to. In bed mostly.
It's my dad, standing in the door frame
not entering – but pausing to shape advice
that keeps coming back. "Whatever is matter,

must *enjoy the life*." He pronounced this twice.
And me, I heard wrongness in putting a *the*

before *life*. In two minds. Ashamed. Aware.
That I knew better, though was stuck inside
while the sun was out. That I'm native here
In a halfway house. Like that sticking word.
That definite article, half right, half
wrong, still present between *enjoy* and *life*.

Zaffar Kunial

PARSING THE POEM

When we read "The Word," the phrase that stuck out was "enjoy the life," as it did for the author when his father inappropriately inserted a "the" in between "enjoy" and "life." This made us smile. We had each mentioned in our check-in that we could use a lighter topic after the more emotional writing of previous weeks. It was no surprise when the online-writing prompt that arose was "Think of a time when you deviated from 'the life' and enjoyed it." What we wrote reflected the humor we found in the phrase. It was an entertaining exercise. We have not included the online stories in this chapter; suffice it to say that Penny told of a time she got on the wrong train and Darcy wrote about a diminutive but much-loved car he and his wife had early in their careers.

This lighthearted writing led us to more profound questions as we revisited the poem and created a prompt for our at-home writing.

THE QUEST FOR AN INVITING WRITING PROMPT

In creating prompts, we invite you to follow your heart without forcing. It may surprise you! Notice what comes to light, what else wants to be said, what new question is ready to be explored. Revisiting a writing prompt may spark different aspects of memory and exploration, especially if it is a prompt that seems juicy for both of you. You just don't know what will emerge when you start to write! The mind has a hidden store of memories, and writing often lets you in. The important thing is to hold it lightly—if more wants to come, let it. Some digging is just digging. Some digging hits veins of gold.

After reading our online stories to each other, we again looked at the poem for potential questions for our at-home writing over the next week. Words like "halfway house," "stuck," and "in between" moved us into more nuanced territory. We now felt ready for another deep dive. What emerged was, "What are you betwixt and between and what serves as a halfway house?" It drew both of us to explore some hard but universal truths like life, death, and loss. The stories went to some tough places for both of us.

We felt the beckoning call of this prompt. At each life stage, for each season, in every day, we are required to make peace with the uncertainty that is part of life. We must find ways to hold the tension between what is and what will be, what is known and what is yet unknown, what is hard and what is joyful. It might be the most difficult thing that is asked of us; to just wait and see. We are beholden to the trickle of time. It was a compelling invitation to consider this question in its particularity at this moment in our lives.

WRITING AS A PATH TO MEANING-MAKING

As we worked with the poems and writing prompts that arose, we found they didn't sit still on the page. They kept working on us even though we weren't working on them. Like a pebble dropped in a pool, ripples go out, but they also bounce back when they meet a shoreline or other boundary.

The process of organizing this book took us further into our stories and lives. Those reflected ripples led to what follows our stories in this and subsequent chapters—new thoughts, additional memories, and newly discovered connections and meanings. The additional material gives more context and texture to what we started in our year of writing.

PENNY AT-HOME
What are you betwixt and between and what serves as a halfway house?

What rises to the top is Life and Death—I am so very alive yet at 80 I am also aware in a poignant way that death is the next largest of all transitions. Since it is not yet impinging, it would be easy to deny or ignore this final doorway. Yet it is the very acknowledgment of death and making it conscious that creates the need for and comfort in a halfway house.

What serves as a place of grounding, as a state of being, in between these two gates? It is more than one thing: it is coming back to the present moment and living "awake to each day"; it is appreciating with gratitude all that unfolds in each day—in meditation, in loving David, in these spring walks with flowers and people in full bloom. It is laughter, it is the routines of cooking, it is the anticipation of upcoming travel. This isn't so very different from other times in my life, come to think of it. But it is more precious now, and the lurking fear when yet another friend becomes sick or dies reminds me that the distance from Betwixt to Between is narrowing all the time.

What else is there to do but love what I love and give my all to it, to dwell in the spacious abundance in which I find myself and not to take any of it for granted? My connections with beloved friends and family are another source of solace and grounding. I know myself through relationships, listening and making sense and meaning in the conversations I have—holding and weaving our life stories in a many-stranded tapestry over time. Each time I have a rich conversation with my daughter, with dear friends, with coaching clients or other colleagues, I come back home to myself. All of these stories make up my world and in some ways are fractals of "the world." I feel honored and lucky to have friends of all ages so that the stories span different life stages and the transitions, struggles and joys of each stage—the wedding of a young friend, the return of a serious illness in an older friend, the birthday of my 16-year-old step-granddaughter, the new business venture of my 52-year-old daughter and her husband, the vibrancy of my age-mates—this is my world.

I was glad to realize the other day how comfortable I am to be in my own body, at my own age, an appreciative observer of others: young men and women sculling on the Schuylkill River each morning, for instance. I love the beauty of youthful, athletic bodies even as I am okay with my own slower, softer, less lithe (lithe-less, not lifeless) body!

There is a middle-aged (maybe 40-year-old) cleaning person in our apartment building. When I introduced myself to her about a month after we had moved in, she blurted out that she had seen me and my partner. She said that all she could think of was the life we must have lived and that we would be dead soon. She said she wanted to see her son grow up before she died. This was so unexpected and could have been off-putting except for my quirky sense of humor that made me laugh internally at her bluntness. Ever since then I have referred to her (to myself) as "she who thinks I'll be dead soon." Not yet.

ON REFLECTION . . .

PENNY
Beneath the First Layer of Truth-Telling

In writing about being betwixt and between, I wrested myself out of a spate of recent losses and encroaching fears. I turned towards what is life-giving. That is my nature. Yet is it enough to whisper brave words (we all die, friends have died) and then run back into my preferred safe harbor of focusing on life? Where is the healthy balance? I see that this first layer of writing has barely acknowledged what is just beneath the surface. Now, upon rereading what I wrote, I am called to go further. I must do more than name the hard realities of this time in my life in a peremptory way. I need to feel them in my bones.

Beneath the truth of my aliveness and happiness lives a pool of sadness. My dear friend's husband died two days ago after a long and painful illness. She was full of the held-back floods of tears that she had barely shown during these last years. Now they are a river. I feel bathed by the cleansing of them and join her with my own tears on our Zoom call of grief—she being in another city.

My oldest college friend died two weeks ago. She kept her illness a secret and only told me how sick she was days before she died. It was her way. She announced that she was "done" and ready to go (cancer having metastasized everywhere). We had a last conversation (I didn't know it then) about our boy-friends at 17. The next day she was placed on a morphine drip and we never talked again.

And yesterday, horrifyingly, a young friend who just had a baby after years of trying wrote to say that she had almost died in childbirth. She was my antidote to aging—a healthy vibrant woman just starting this phase of her life. I stretch to hold her in my heart. I cannot bear it, but I do.

And me—so often impervious to pain and feeling so fit—now with my own challenging neck injury. Perhaps my unspoken sadness and unnamed fears have taken up resi-dence in my body. Physical therapy is a welcome and necessary reality. I am glad for the help and angry about the pain. There. I've said it. I have admitted the worst and spoken the impolite truths. They are on my road too. I am determined that I will not turn into a fearful sad complainer. I will not. Yet it feels important to let in the reality of the other side of betwixt and between—the harder side.

PENNY
Writing as a Portal to Courage

Upon rereading what I wrote in my first response to our at-home question, I was called to delve further, to do more than simply name the myriad losses of this time of life, to feel them as reality. There is a way in which saying brave words made me think I'd faced the abyss. But I realized that can be a trap. I talked about death as the next transition. But until I wrote the details, the immediacy of it, I didn't completely let it in. Now I have and my body has softened. Grief is a whole-body experience. Having let myself be here, I don't need to stay. I can hold beauty and pain, love and loss, and surprisingly to do so is both a relief and a release—in fact, it is a necessity.

Writing opens me to write more, especially when I read what I've written aloud to Darcy and he doesn't flinch or run away. It emboldens me to go to the hardest places; not to dwell there but to take in the whole of life so that I can live in the full reality of love and loss. I am learning that writing allows me to discover where I am in the moment. I can come back again and again to find out if there is more to write—more to say, more to feel. I can be brave on these pages.

DARCY AT-HOME
What are you betwixt and between and what serves as a halfway house?

Charlie is betwixt and between and because he is, we are too. He was diagnosed with laryngeal cancer 16 months ago. Following surgical debulking and a brief course of chemotherapy, he has been doing wonderfully. Eating well, playing, and being his exceptionally affectionate self. However, dark clouds are on the horizon. Some snuffling and sneezing are making me suspicious the cancer has returned and set up housekeeping in his nose.

Shelley and I have been in the your-cat-is-going-to-die-sooner-rather-than-later waiting room since January 2022. Waiting for the other shoe to drop. For the cancer to return, and lymphoma almost always does. Charlie has been a lucky cat. To have another 16-and-however-more months tacked onto his kitty life is pretty good, all things considered. We have been lulled into a state of hopefulness. Maybe, just maybe it won't come back. Charlie's imminent demise fell below the surface for a while. A happy respite, but now real worries return.

There is a special burden that all pet owners implicitly assume when they choose to have a pet. We get to decide all things about their well-being, whether we want to or are ready to. Singular among those is choosing when and how they die, unless that is taken out of your hands by an accident or other circumstances. Most consider their pets to be a part of the family. Special unique spirits that join us for a brief time on our collective journeys. With us through the hard times and good. A nonjudgmental source of solace and companionship who are happy just to be with us whoever we are. Pretty, ugly, overweight, thin, rich, poor, selfish, generous, homeless, or not.

When the end of their lives looms, we must quiet ourselves, look into their eyes, and decide. Is now the right time? How are you feeling? Have you suffered enough? How much is too much? Am I holding on for me or for you? What if I make the wrong decision? Can I live with the decision I've made? It can tear your heart open, and sometimes out altogether.

The uncertain and fragile space between now and then, however, is lit by a warm glow like the last swelling bloom shed by an expiring candle. We hold them, pet them, and watch closely. Sometimes looking for answers to the bleak questions facing us but mostly, just to appreciate them. Moment by moment and day by day. No expectations, no looking too far ahead. We feed them anything. No fancy or expensive treat goes unbought. We throw the ball, dangle the string, or hide the toy mouse under the blanket just the way they like it. This is the halfway house.

The temporary shelter before we go out into the sadness that lies ahead. We pull down the blinds on our worries for a time. This is a hallowed space. A tender space. A space where we build a mental cradle to hold them in until the end. Until the last breath, stroke, and whispered tenderness. Until the light in their eyes dims and drifts away into our hearts forever. (P.S. We said goodbye to our sweet boy July 21, 2024. RIP Charlie).

ON REFLECTION . . .

DARCY
Naming and Holding the Tension

There are currents ebbing and flowing in the background of my inner life that I'm frequently not quite aware of, and yet, can and do affect the way I show up to the outside world and to myself. I'm often holding tensions about something that can be big or small with short- or long-term implications. Writing opens a space for me to name these tensions and explore them. I could, of course, just sit and think about it, but writing pulls something extra out of me. A strange alchemy is at work in the way it draws more honesty, clarity, and insight out of the blurry base elements that exist in my present moments.

The question on betwixt and between that Penny and I wrote about revealed present, below-the-surface tensions we were holding. For me, it was about my much-loved and not-well cat, Charlie. For Penny, it was looking at the big existential inevitability that awaits us all, death.

Penny and I chat more about "enjoy the life" and are both drawn to respond to it. On the surface, it seems like a presumptuous, self-satisfied, simple exhortation, but there is complexity here. It needs to be peeled back layer by layer and the words parsed. What do you mean by "the life?" What do you mean by "enjoy?" It's complicated and, like answers to most hard questions, it depends. I took a look at it from two sides.

DARCY
Enjoy THE Life?

"The Word," or as I see it, "THE Word." It makes me chuckle when I think of the title of Zaffar Kunial's poem. It implies there really is only one special word among the panoply of pretenders. A word that is whispered to those in the "I know something you don't" club. Opener of doors, granter of wishes, explainer of all things, mono- or multisyllabic, it doesn't matter because it's *the* word. A word to rule them all.

Clients would tell me their dog has *the* diarrhea. Not ordinary diarrhea, but *the* diarrhea, a special, malodorous malady ripe with drama, mystery, and malintent! Crowning a word, any word, with "the" shines a hallowed light on it. When you double down and put "the" before "life" and then throw gasoline on it by placing "enjoy" before it all—well, you've kicked the existential hornet's nest, and for good measure, picked it up and put it in your pocket. This preamble is my way of avoiding direct, head-on engagement with that troublesome and inviting phrase in the poem "enjoy the life."

DARCY
One Side—Delight Discovered

When I was 17, I went to Hawaii with my parents. That was the place to go for most Western Canadians wanting a break from winter in the 1970s, and still is, for that matter. My mother and father were starting to figure out how to coexist with each other and stay married after a horrible prior few years. This was a period of détente for them; emotional knives were put away for the time being. We were going to Hawaii!

This was a big trip for my father, who had never been on an overseas flight, and out of this world for me, as this was my first ride on an airplane and first experience of a tropical environment. Unbelievably exotic for a kid who grew up on the flat, dusty prairies of Western Canada. There were so many firsts.

The warm embrace of humid tropical air. How the sun went down so fast with no extended twilight that I had come to know living in a northern latitude. When it rained, as it often did later in the day, it wasn't bad at all. A warm bath, not freezing cold. Your clothes dried quickly when the sun came back out shortly thereafter. How cool is that?

Everything smelled like coconuts. A fragrance I like, but it was mostly from the coconut-scented tanning oil that was the rage back then. People slathered it on and baked (or rather basted) in the sun all day. An innocent time before the risk of skin cancer and its link to ultraviolet radiation became widely known. I also discovered that surfing was fun and very hard. Countless times I was buried by waves on Waikiki Beach, getting tumbled into and scraped by sharp coral only to emerge to see my surfboard happily riding a wave to shore without me. I loved every minute of it.

One memory stands out amidst all this fun. It shifted my preconceptions so much that I still think about it often. Don't worry, I did not discover my purpose in life or come to understand why we exist. Afterall, I was just 17. What I did learn was that the truth of things is, well, complicated, and it depends. In my case, the teacher was a pineapple. Let me explain.

Growing up, the only pineapple I had eaten was from a can. I was not a fan. It tasted like the tin can it was stored in. We used to put it on pizza along with ham. In Western Canada, this is known as the Hawaiian pizza and is very popular. The combination of melted cheese, fresh yeasty dough, and the salt-sweet contrast between the ham and pineapple pushed all the right gustatory buttons. I loved Hawaiian pizzas despite the canned pineapple.

As I was walking down the main drag adjacent to Waikiki Beach, there were all sorts of shops selling fresh pineapple. I thought, *I'm here, I should try it.* The first bite paralyzed me. The tender, sweet slab of pineapple stuck out of my mouth, and juice ran down my chin. This was an epiphany, the first I can remember. Never did I imagine that pineapple could taste like this. Sweet and soft, with a fibrous crunchiness and acidity that made your mouth come alive.

Over the course of the week, I'm sure I ate my body weight in fresh pineapple. That was the good part. The challenging part was a voice in the back of my head that was getting louder and louder. It was saying "Darcy, if you were so wrong about the truth of pineapple, how many other truths are you wrong about?" This gut-filling but mind-bending surprise was the first of many that turned out, time and time again, to be my most profound teachers. "The life" has been a never-ending series of surprises, good and bad.

DARCY
Beliefs Held

Another surprise upended a long-held belief that life is linear and somewhat predictable. On the whole, it is from a biological perspective. Time goes by day by day, year by year, and we age—some faster than others but the progression is inevitable. The life of the heart and soul (overlooked in my earlier calculations), however, is nothing close to linear. It goes up and down, this way and that, swerves right then left, and where it ends up is a mystery. It does not lend itself to quantitative analysis.

The heart and soul can't be added, subtracted, divided, or multiplied. They can be hard to know and are ever so unpredictable! I hate it and love it. This truth caught up with me in my early forties. (Yes, it took me a while to mature!). I was primed early on for all the delights and interesting surprises that life brought me—that's one side. The other and darker side I didn't count on. The one full of loss and sorrow. How do you carry it? How to hold it without getting consumed by it? I didn't know how to grieve.

DARCY
The Other Side—A Loss Lived

The tipping point was the death of my father. What started with a heart attack in his early forties progressed to a triple bypass and aortic valve replacement in his seventies. Several years later, congestive heart failure set in and finally reached its predictable end. I used to phone home every Sunday and talk to my parents. My father's frequent episodes of moist coughing that broke up our conversations were a telltale sign of uncontrolled pulmonary edema due to heart failure. Something I was very familiar with in my dog and cat patients.

I got the call in late April. Dad was not doing well and had been transferred to a palliative care unit in a nursing home mere blocks away from our family home in Moose Jaw. I flew home from Prince Edward Island. My sister, Debbie, who had already arrived from Calgary, met me at the Regina Airport. She shared recent developments about my father as we drove the 40 well-worn miles west to Moose Jaw. We soon settled into silence, each of us processing the new reality.

For the next three days, my mother, Debbie, and I visited him daily. He was semi-conscious and unable to converse. I'm sure he knew we were present but there was no opportunity for a final exchange of favorite stories, exclamations about the state of the world, or laughs about something ludicrous.

We sat, watched him struggle to breathe, and waited. Taut and poised, stalled in a time outside of time, waiting for the next downward lurch. The telephone rang at 2 am. Debbie and I were sleeping in basement bedrooms. We both heard the ring and creak of the floor above us as our mother walked to the kitchen to pick up the phone. Debbie and I knew this was it, got up, dressed, and went upstairs. The nurse had called to let us know the end was near.

We waited in the living room for Mom to get dressed. Time passed and she had not emerged. What was taking her so long? Just as we were about to check, she appeared wearing a well-appointed jacket and skirt, make-up on and hair done. Yes, of course. Our mother was of the generation that never went out into public looking unprepared or underdressed. It was her uniform, her suit of armor to support her for the experience ahead.

We sit by my dad's bedside for the next two hours. His breathing is labored and irregular. Every ragged inhale is followed by a sharp, perfunctory exhale, as if his body is saying, "There, I did it, one more breath." A long silence follows. Is this his last breath? Please let it be. He has struggled enough. Eventually the last one comes.

We sit silently and look at my father, quiet, still, body systems shutting down, spirit dissipating. We get up and hug each other in a huddle of three. It's over. Relief and loss linger. Although I had seen many animals die, I had never been with a human being in their last moments, let alone a close family member. A searing experience that lodged inside me only to re-emerge in the future as another life-changing surprise. Ten years later my heart opens, and I start crying. I've come to call those intervening years the lost decade. Time wasn't lost, but I was. A story for later.

DARCY
Considering the Whole

That brings me back to "enjoy the life." I'm not sure I could say I have wholeheartedly enjoyed it. Gratitude rather than enjoyment feels closer to home. Understanding that suffering and loss have as much, or more, to teach me as joy and happiness continues to be true (and is still a struggle). I'm grateful to have grown up, especially on the inside, to be a decent human being. If I took an open, expansive view of enjoyment, then yes, I've "enjoyed the life," but I'm surprised at how tricky it turned out to be.

SOME CLOSING THOUGHTS

PENNY
Choosing Life

"What else is there to do but love what I love and give my all to it, to dwell in the spacious abundance in which I find myself and not take any of it for granted?" When I reread the words I penned about my life now, I am drawn to a reflective place. Has it always been so? These 52 weeks of writing give me a way to make a new kind of meaning of the tapestry of events, choices, inner qualities, and learned capacities that have shaped who I am.

I see that "enjoy the life" is not a steady state. It is a choice, again and again. These stories include moments as well as sweeps of time. I see the lay of the land more clearly: how I have fallen into dark holes and chosen life, how I have found my gifts and flourished; how I have felt alienated and also felt I belonged, and how I have created spaces for others to find their voice and their path. I have found myself again and again (which means of course that I have lost my way as well). It happens in connection with others, in nature, in music, in art, and in love—always in love—given and received. And in this year of writing, it has happened most poignantly with a friend. Meaning-making is not a solo event. With our writing and sharing, Darcy and I affirm and welcome each other into discoveries of meaning.

Some years ago, I attended a workshop where we were invited to tell our life story to a partner in five different ways: as a romance, a tragedy, a grand adventure, a mystery, and a heroic tale. It was great fun to do, and it was more than that. It struck me that how we tell our story (to ourselves or others) has a lot to do with how we live our lives. We always have a choice. I look back and realize that I have (at each juncture) had an appetite for loving life, for finding my way to give what I have, and then to love what I love, and give my all to it. Even when in despair, ultimately, I chose life— each time. My inner dialogue went something like: "Damned if I'll give up on this precious life with all that is possible. If you don't love it, find some part you can connect with, and if that doesn't work, leave and discover something you do love." Life taught me that losing myself was always too high a price to pay. Perhaps this is my version of claiming that I "must enjoy the life."

PENNY
Being a Bridge

Being often an outsider led me to create communities in which I too could belong. I realized somewhat intuitively that I could "enjoy the life" by becoming a bridge for others instead of trying to fit into a mold that didn't work for me. In work and personal life, I have searched for ways and places in which I could flourish as my authentic self and invite others in. In reaching to give others what I lacked, I created safe homes. Ironically, I learned to open my own heart and bare (bear) my own vulnerability by inviting others to do so and finding the courage to reciprocate. I am grateful that I never give up believing that life and love, learning and opening to the mystery are always possible.

Over time, I learned more about loving myself for who I am, with all my imperfections and gifts, stumbling and gracefulness. Ultimately, the possibility for me to "enjoy the life" rested on this capacity. I say that easily now, but it was a hard won and still ongoing journey. Anything less was too often akin to "being stuck inside while the sun was out." Here's the story that turned things around for me.

PENNY
A Fateful Choice

I was in a 10-day silent meditation retreat when I was nearly 60 (I wish it had been even sooner, but perhaps these things happen when the soil is prepared and not before). I had been plagued by various anxieties even while feeling the immense gifts of the life I was living and work I was doing. I couldn't seem to relax into self-acceptance; always on the alert for not being enough. My whole being knew I needed uninterrupted silence, having been in a grueling schedule of weekly travel and work, all involving constant interactions and connection with others. I craved quiet—time to make sense of what I was living and hopefully to find some respite from my gnawing sense of apprehensiveness.

Ten days is a long time to be silent. We were in the desert of southern California. Each day was a mix of sitting and walking meditation. I loved walking in the little oasis, where I came to know which flowers were about to bloom. I made friends with a bee, watching it for many minutes as it flew from blossom to blossom. Meals were silent. I felt the outer world dropping away, yet instead of feeling a dissipation of anxiety, I felt its sharp edge without the buffer of distractions. On the sixth day, each retreat participant had a 20-minute meeting with one of the teachers in which to share anything we wished. I met with Jack Kornfield, the senior guide for the retreat. I had learned so much from his writing and was glad to have been assigned to him.

When you only have 20 minutes, there's no time for small talk. I plunged in and said what was sitting on my heart—how my life included so much that was fulfilling and yet I was plagued with anxiety. Jack asked me if I practiced *metta*, a lovingkindness meditation where you wish safety, peace, happiness, care, and love for those you love or like, those you don't know, those you don't like, and for yourself. When I said I did, he asked how much of the time I wished those blessings for myself. Not much, I replied. He invited me for the remaining four days to practice metta for myself for an unthinkable 90% of my meditating. I was surprised, as it felt so self-serving, but agreed to do it—to turn the love I gave to others back to myself in the days of meditation practice that followed.

Here is what happened. In one of the meditations, I visualized myself sitting by the side of a stream. I had many arms, like an octopus. I was peaceful until one of my anxious voices piped up and said, "You're not living up to your potential." I felt one of my arms wrap around that voice and felt myself say, "Oh, you're not so bad, honey." Another voice piped up, "You're too fat." Again, another of my arms cradled that voice and said, "You're okay, kiddo." It went on like that, me sitting by the stream with my many loving arms cradling each sad, fearful, angry, self-judging voice, until I was embracing all of me and felt loving towards every part. I experienced a seismic shift, and sensed it would last, going forward. My job wasn't to fix myself; it was to love myself. I had been teaching this very thing to others. Finally, now, I felt its reality from the inside out.

I have changed. I cannot change back.
I have come this far forever.

Joseph Campbell

CHAPTER FIVE

Words and Beyond Words

Words create worlds, and our senses do too. In this chapter, we take a stroll with some favorite words after having been piqued by the poem "Bullshit" by Vahni (Anthony) Capildeo. A powerful, pejorative, in-your-face (not literal in most cases, although it has been in Darcy's veterinary work) word. The poet begins with "How to 'lose' or 'abandon' a word? Put it in jail, throw away the key?"

That was enough to get us started, and for our online writing, we turned it around to write about a word or words we loved instead. What arises from a poem to form a prompt may be just one word or a short phrase, as was the case here.

Many times, we framed a question for our online writing that was lighthearted, playful, or evoked amusing memories or flights of fancy. Such was the situation on this day, when we turned to words we loved in response to our online writing prompt, "What word do you like to roll around in your mouth like sweet candy?" Honestly, how we got from bullshit to rolling something around in our mouths like sweet candy is a mystery, but the counterpoint made it an even funnier prompt for us to play with.

It is part of the gift of our friendship that we can sort so easily what questions want to be explored at different times. It is a mark of the trust and respect between us that we navigated our writing journey with such attentiveness and candor. We came into the shallows when needed and returned to depths or heights as a predictable dance.

PENNY ONLINE
What word do you like to roll around in your mouth like sweet candy?

Two words jump into my mouth to be "rolled": luscious and lascivious. The first is all pleasure. Luscious sounds like what it is—delightful, round, tasty, enticing. I like the feel of the word. It conjures up what it is speaking of—a fantastical dessert like English trifle, or a soft fluffy duvet where you can snuggle down under and be wrapped in luxurious warmth.

The second brings a sneer. Lascivious calls up not-so-lovely images of cads and lechers and creepy men on dark streets. Yet it is wonderful to say—also conjuring up precisely what it means. I feel plunged into a story when I say "lascivious"; a tale of horror, a thriller. Nothing good can come of this. Yet oh, what forbidden pleasure it is to toss it off my tongue after it has rolled around. "He was downright lascivious"—not a favorable way to name someone's behavior, yet so descriptive.

Can you be luscious and lascivious at the same time? Not likely. More like "the lascivious man licked his lips at the sight of the luscious young woman." It is very Victorian and makes me smile. In 2023 one hopes the luscious female would bop the lascivious male on the head—an old-fashioned response to arcane descriptors.

I think of grade school where we were taught the meaning of words by using them in a sentence. Lascivious was never one of those words. Luscious might have been.

DARCY ONLINE
What word do you like to roll around in your mouth like sweet candy?

I heard it first in my second-year veterinary parasitology class. It stuck with me in a way that parasites stick to us and other animals. Embedded, implanted, persistent. The genus and species name of this parasite is *Diphyllobothrium latum*. It is common and known as the fish tapeworm. Dogs and people get infected by eating raw fish. It can grow up to 30 feet long in humans. Pretty impressive!

The word "Diphyllobothrium" [di-file-o-both-ree-umm] rolls off the tongue with a certain phonetic cadence that delights. It has an upper-crust, high-class kind of enunciation. It could fit right in during a post-dinner conversation over a glass of port in a stately English country home. "Diphylloboth-rium" pronounced with confidence or outrage could describe how you feel about the state of the nation or of a proposed salt tax. Alternatively, it could be used when quizzical or surprised. "Well, *Diphyllobothrium*, my dear!"

I think the reason this phonetically attractive word has lingered is that this seemingly upright and upstanding term describes a parasite—one that lives in an unmentionable place (at least in polite company—get a group of veterinarians together though, and well, you can imagine) and is associated with questionable eating habits. Sadly, parasitologists (too much time on their hands, if you ask me) have now changed the name to *Dibothriocephalus*, not nearly as pleasing. I'll stick to the old ways. So, "*Diphyllobothrium*, my good man," may you never meet me!

OUR LIGHT-HEARTED FORAY

We had fun writing about a marvelously named parasite and an unlikely pair of words.

[A note from Penny: I delight in Darcy's scientific bent and notice he often includes the Latin names (genus and species) of the organisms he talks about. It is so natural to him that it was a surprise when I mentioned it. I am enchanted by his distinctive take on life and often bemused by the resulting differences in our approach to questions.]

These lighter first writings made us laugh. They relaxed us and opened the door to creativity and depth when we crafted our prompt for at-home writing. We turned to the flip side of words in creating our second question: "Think of an experience that took you beyond words." It led us each to a place of awe and wonder where the power of words alone cannot capture an experience, but another power can.

WORDLESS WISDOM THAT LIVES IN THE BODY

Words can be poor conduits to truly understand an experience. We have to feel it in our bodies—or in our bones, as the saying goes—to fully comprehend it. We have to touch, hear it, smell it, or see it. Our whole body needs to be plunged into the experience. When it is, it remembers.

Both of us are fascinated and humbled by what our bodies hold and communicate to us. Frederich Nietzsche said that "There is more wisdom in your body than in your deepest philosophy." Most of us tend to take our bodies for granted and live largely in our heads, assuming our bodies will look after the necessities and keep us going. That is, until they don't, and we grumpily wonder why. More often than not, they have been sending us messages that we ignored.

An acupuncturist that Darcy goes to is fond of saying, "Issues live in the tissues." Not only do old physical injuries come back to burden us, but past small and big "T" emotional trauma does as well. The area of mind-body medicine has exploded over the last couple of decades as the scope and significance of the connections emerge. Based on the scientific research, many think the Western philosophical notion of a separate mind and body is a fallacy. Eastern philosophies have never separated the two.

PENNY
Prelude

When we created this question, "Think of an experience that took you beyond words," I had just booked tickets to Paris for the following spring and was primed to remember my first, long-ago trip to that beloved city. What surprised me was my embodied recall of being there as a young woman. Paris is a sensual city, and my memories were sensual as well. I had no idea I would recall nuances of touch, sight, hearing, and taste. I could do more than recall the events of my story; I could feel them in my body. To my surprise, I found tears coming as I relived the glorious experience of the concert—over 50 years ago, yet as alive as yesterday. The question to turn beyond words was prescient and reminded me that I am more than my thoughts.

PENNY AT-HOME
Think of an experience that took you beyond words.

I was young, 26 maybe, and in Paris alone for a few days. It was an amazing, eye-opening trip—my first time in this sensual city—sights, tastes, sounds, little connections with strangers, short interchanges in my primitive French, my first real croissant, the Rodin Museum, the Musée D'Orsay, the Seine, the walks along sidewalks on the Left Bank where artists sold their sketches and paintings. I was taking it all in and storing it up; no one to exclaim to or share it with, but later, oh the stories I would have.

On this particular night, I had bought the last ticket to a performance with Itzhak Perlman who was to play the Brahms Violin Concerto, one of my favorites. The ticket was in the first row, center orchestra. I'd be craning my neck, but I didn't care. I was in Paris. The closer, the better. I'd been listening to Perlman on my record (!) but had never seen him live. I was so excited.

When Perlman entered the stage in his wheelchair, I was stunned. How could I not have known he was paralyzed?

How could he be such an exuberant spirit of a man? How had he risen to these heights as a violinist? How could this be?

He smiled broadly and then settled into a serious expression as he lifted the violin to his chin and took up his bow. All my thoughts quieted as he began to play. He was so close to me, I could almost have touched his hand. I was lost. The music surrounded me, engulfed me, became me. Even when a string broke and he continued playing on the remaining strings while fastening a new one in place, even then the spell of his playing, of the music, held. It held, and it held me entranced.

The chatter in my head ceased. I was beyond words in the way great music can do—swept into the pure connection with the mystery, my heart's longing, life's poignancy and beauty, and this man, this mortal man—struck by polio at age four (I later read), the conduit of joy from then to now: from the timeless past, from the life of Johannes Brahms creating this concerto, to me, a young woman excited to be in Paris listening to magic.

It was late, maybe midnight, when I left to find my way back to my inexpensive hotel. I was on a strict budget taken directly from *Europe on 5 Dollars a Day* in an era when that was possible. I would have to walk home, a cab being beyond me and the Metro closed for the night. A young French couple somehow sensed my circumstances and gave me a lift to my hotel. I spoke so little French and they spoke no English. We were heady from the performance and all we could say all the way to my hotel was "incroyable." I was content not to be able to say more. I was beyond words.

It makes me tear up to remember that night, looking back over 50-plus years—to reawaken not "words" but the embodied memory of awe and beauty still alive in me. At the end of the concert, Itzhak Perlman bowed from his wheelchair to a standing ovation and rolled himself, with joy, off the stage.

DARCY AT-HOME
Think of an experience that took you beyond words.

I took the socks off my hands (cold day, forgotten gloves) and touched it. Fingers splayed, whole palm pressed against the spongy, moist, terra-cotta-colored fibrous coating. The protective skin that has covered this monument and its kin for centuries. Kept it safe from the ravages of fire and other assaults. I breathed in the cool mountain air scented with earth, wood, and life. I was surrounded by it. Time and perseverance stood in front of me. Soaring to over two hundred feet—and in this grove, none are younger than a thousand years.

Sequoiadendron giganteum, or giant sequoia, inhabit a small area high in the Sierra Nevada mountains of southern California. The misty mountain environment suits them. It's a small area and there are not many sequoias left. They have stood for centuries, resolute, whispering to the wind and birds and to whomever else might listen. Holding, guarding a deep wisdom that we may never know. Even the most jaded human being becomes silent in their presence. Because there is something sacred here. It doesn't need a voice or words to bring it into being. You breathe it in, the aromas fill your nose, and your feet feel the weight of this place. It's important. It's special. It's showing us we don't have all the wisdom, and maybe none at all. We feel humbled and insignificant among these giants. A good thing for an ego-driven, self-obsessed species such as ourselves! They don't mean to do that, of course, but what else can we feel when truth stands in front of us? They exist for their own purposes. They show us that there are different ways of being in this world and that the earth is not all ours to do with as we will.

So we stand in silence and bow our heads in awe and respect. We might even pray because this is the original cathedral. This is my cathedral. It calls us to see what life on this planet really is. The heartbeat and rhythm we all move to. Honor this and we honor ourselves as we step into the hard, heartbreaking, and joyful work we have as thoughtful stewards of this world we call home.

ARISING FROM THE DEEP— MORE MEMORIES, MORE STORIES

One of the lessons we learned over our year of writing was to intentionally create some of our writing prompts around the full array of senses—music, dance, touch, color, taste, and so on—in addition to the natural focus on thoughts, words. Worlds of stored sensations and memories are unleashed with the right prompt. Kind of like an array of open, honest questions that invite the listener to access different aspects of their knowing. It is a mysterious lock-and-key kind of deal, where the right key can unlock whole storerooms of treasure. It's another way of meaning-making, discovering our own truth through the way that nature, art, music, and other immersive experiences touch us in a variety of ways.

Because we could not let this rich topic go, below we share further memories and stories evoked by an additional prompt: "What other embodied memories involving words or physical sensations arise?"

PENNY
What other embodied memories involving words or physical sensations arise?

When I reread my Paris story, it sent me into a reflective place, realizing that both music and body-knowing have been threads woven throughout my life. I share some of those reflections below. For both Darcy and me, bringing up these experiences was another vital way to understand our lives. Nature, art, music, and movement are important players in our stories and worthy of attention. Perhaps it will be that way for you as well. We invite you to see.

PENNY
Memories of Music

I grew up listening to my mother playing the Steinway concert grand piano that was the centerpiece of our living room. The notes filled me, were a natural part of my environment the way water is for fish. She practiced for hours every day: Beethoven sonatas, Bach preludes, Debussy aires, all the classical masters. She taught piano to children and adults, also in our living room. In the evenings, Papa and Mama played classical records. There was music all the time.

And I danced in the evenings. At five or six, I would ask for "The Carnival of the Animals," marvelous work by Saint-Saens, and move my little body in faster and faster spins and turns, keeping pace with the mood and rhythms of the music. I loved that feeling of expressing myself through the notes.

I had to be very still when Mama was practicing. This was a serious business, going over and over the same passages until her fingers flew and the notes were a seamless stream of melody and chords and pure feeling. I wasn't really supposed to be in the room at all. So I made myself very small and sat curled up next to the right front leg of the piano, like a little snail. From there I could see the undersides of her hands as they flew up and down the keys, fingers curved to carry the soul of the music. (She always emphasized how the heart of the piece came through rounded fingers. Straight fingers resulted in a harsh, technical rendering; no heart. Later, when I played the piano myself, this image rang in my mind. I always curved my fingers!)

I felt the music and it was like being held by my mother. She gave her music as much love as she gave me. It was how I knew her—focused, mouth set in concentration, fingers held just so, and the magic of Mendelssohn or Chopin streaming out.

My mother had performed on stage for several years, most notably at Town Hall, an impressive venue in New York City, second only to Carnegie Hall. I don't remember that. The combination of performance anxiety and having one and then two of us children to raise ended her concertizing. Even then she continued to practice every day and I was her audience, as were my father and friends who came for dinner and an evening of music. When I close my eyes I can still see and hear her playing. Most exciting was when she played a "large" work, like a Beethoven concerto. Then she raised the top of the Steinway, held open by the dowel that propped up the massive side. The vibrations of the notes melded with the sounds—a total body experience.

Once a month, Mama had a piano lesson with Mr. Rutko. She often brought me with her to his apartment to sit while she played and was guided, corrected, and praised. Mr. Rutko hugged me hello each time. I hated that part because he smelled like tuna fish. I wondered why she needed more lessons. To me she was already perfect, sounding just like our records.

Mr. Rutko's son Peter was a concert pianist. I heard stories of how he practiced for 12 or 13 hours every day, sometimes without eating. This seemed to be a good thing, one that my mom aspired to. Hearing those stories, I sometimes felt in the way, an obstacle to her unending desire to perfect her playing.

I learned about the opposing pulls of motherhood and passion for a profession in those years. Without ever talking about it, I took in the importance and challenge of trying to do both. I didn't like sharing her, but it was reality. (Later, I experienced those same pulls as I balanced caring for my daughter with carving out a life of meaning through work).

PENNY
Threads of Embodied Knowing

Movement is life! When I was a little kid, I felt everything in my body. My body had to move and knew how it wanted to move. When I danced for my parents, I twirled and lost myself in the beauty of melody, rhythm, and feeling. In Central Park, my Manhattan playground blocks from our apartment, any grassy hill propelled me to roll down it (always more appealing in my mind's eye than in reality—which was often bumpy and a bit painful). A particular sloping pavement was an invitation to roller skate, awaiting the moment when I could let go and glide. My memory is of a mountain-steep grade. I'm pretty sure it was the smallest of inclines (my mom not being physically agile and fearful of accidents). Yet what I remember is the feeling of standing at the top of the hill and being both exhilarated and scared, then letting go—flying!

When I was happy, I jumped or skipped—full of energy and life. When I tried to do something that was hard for me, I put my whole body into it. I have a photo of me at about four blowing a bubble gum bubble with a look of fierce concentration and clenched fists. I even remember throwing myself on the ground in a full-out tantrum when frustrated. At that age, my body-knowing unashamedly integrated my feelings and actions.

At six, I took my first modern dance class with Mama's friend Jane, who had studied with the great Martha Graham. I can still conjure the sensations of leaping and bending to the music with the other little girls. I felt whole. The combination of feeling and moving, sometimes to music, sometimes called from the inside, has always held the key to open my heart to its own knowing.

These early experiences threaded through my life. I get in touch with sadness, joy, longing, love, and life when I move. It is an iterative relationship. When I have been stuck, confused, "in a state," moving helps me know what I feel; recognizing what I am feeling helps me give words to what I think. It opens the doorway to clarity and a path forward.

I went to Antioch College in Yellow Springs, Ohio, where we folk-danced outside every Friday night in a brick courtyard we called Red Square. I can still remember the Salty Dog Rag—hearing the first notes, leaping up to find or be found by a partner and knowing exactly the steps and pauses and swirls that make up this dance. Pure happiness!

I danced at every opportunity—from college through graduate school and into my adulthood. In my thirties and forties, I was a leader and faculty member in an organization devoted to enhancing communication and relational skills for physicians and other health care providers. We traveled the country, leading three- to five-day courses at myriad medical schools. We always built in one evening for dancing and arranged with our hosts to provide live or recorded music. It was a great release and connector. It was part of the glue that bound us, and it leveled the playing field between participants and teachers. No matter how tired we were from long days of work, the music and dancing revived us, released us.

Thich Nhat Hanh (the beloved Tibetan Monk) said, "Your body is your first home." It is a trustworthy guide, ignored at my own peril.

PENNY
A Time of Forgetting. The Power of Remembering

Yet for some years I stopped dancing and became less in touch with how I was feeling. I lost sight of how essential it is for me to express myself through my body. I forgot the connection. My work became all head and no body (except for the meditation that grounded me most mornings and the yoga and walking that kept me fit).

Here is a story of how I remembered again after forgetting. Without quite realizing it, I began looking for some way to bring movement and body-knowing back into my life. I told myself that I was searching on behalf of the participants in the retreats I was leading. (It was easier to see what was missing for others!) While that was true, I was also longing to reconnect with this life-giving connection that had gone underground.

A chance remark from a friend led me to discover my next great teacher (and now dear friend), Arawana Hayashi. When I read about her workshops, which she entitled The Art of Making a True Move, and a more encompassing form she was developing called "Social Presencing Theatre," I knew without question that I had to meet her and experience her work. She used the language of "embodied wisdom," and it resonated. Until then, I hadn't known how to put language to my lifetime experience that my body held a way of knowing that my mind could not access alone.

I will never forget the experience of talking with Arawana on the phone the first time. After a warm and welcoming conversation, I asked if I could spend a few days learning from her. Her schedule of workshop offerings conflicted with my own travel for the year, and I felt a kind of desperation to begin. She graciously agreed, suggesting it would be best to gather a group of at least five people. We set dates for a four-day meeting in her home studio in the Hudson River Valley in upstate New York. I remember saying, "You don't know me, but I want to make sure you are really committing to these dates because when I hang up the phone, I will make this happen." Then I called four friends and excitedly told them of this amazing opportunity. We were all busy professionals, and it was a minor miracle that I immediately connected with each one and they all agreed!! (It was four-year-old me all over again with my fists clenched, metaphorically, and a fierce concentration to make something happen.) We had our plan. I called Arawana back within 45 minutes and told her we were all set. I think she was tickled and amazed. I know I was. It was a fateful beginning of a return to my full self.

That first experience led to my studying with Arawana for two years in a cohort of 22 people, several of whom are still close friends. (You can read more about Arawana's work and Social Presencing Theatre at https://arawanahayashi.com/spt/). Most importantly, I "got it" that I can and must return again and again to the information that is right there for the sensing. It always begins with attention to what the body knows and how we relate to others in this nonverbal practice. It gave me a sustainable way to move forward. I still love to dance to music like I did when I was a little girl, although more slowly now. And I listen to my body voice more often!

DARCY
What other embodied memories involving words or physical sensations arise?

In thinking more about what gets imprinted or entangled in the mind-body, I began to scroll through the words, feelings, images, textures, sounds, and smells within my accumulated memories. I tend to view memories as ethereal vestiges of the past that come and go through the mist. You hold them and they hold you, tenderly, tightly, fiercely, and sometimes, frighteningly. However we hold them, they have a physical presence and leave tracks and trails within our brains. Memories, in neuroscience parlance, are a consequence of changes in gene activation and subsequent protein synthesis mediated by a complex cocktail of chemical neurotransmitters and their cellular receptors. It leads to a continual rewiring of the trillions of connections between the billions of nerve cells (neurons) in our brains.

As it happens, the brain speaks to the body and vice versa. Big time! I'll spare you further exhortations on the specific mechanics of this. Suffice it to say, there is beauty and poetry in this microscopic and molecular conversation. Some memories start in the head and some start in the body. The following was the latter.

DARCY
Something Lost, Something Found

I wake up after a fitful sleep. The room is still dark but near sunrise, confirmed by a glance at the green glow of 6 am on my travel alarm clock. There is a sharp coolness to the air with a scent of wood and mountains. My brain is booting back up, repopulating the current status slots in my wake-up protocol. I am not at home. This is not my bed. I'm in a hotel in a foreign country far from home. I'm participating in a Courage & Renewal retreat in Chile. It's early spring here, late fall at home. Breakfast starts at 8 am and the retreat starts at 9 am. We arrived yesterday as a group at the Nothofagus Hotel in the Huilo Huilo Biological Reserve. Okay, got it.

My feet touch the cold wood floor, made less so by a coarsely woven wool bedside rug. I turn the light on and reacquaint myself with the rustic interior walls made up of wide, rough-sawn, thick vertical planks. I open the drapes and gaze out at the new day unfurling over the wildness of the Patagonian forest.

This retreat is being facilitated by Penny and Deb, a good friend and fellow Courage & Renewal facilitator. It's day one, and I'm excited to be in such a new place. It's my first time in Chile and we just spent a couple of days in the small town of

Pucon, two hours away. Snowcapped dormant volcanoes, crystal clear lakes, and forests of alien-looking Araucaria (monkey puzzle) trees filled our senses.

The first session that morning was about "exploring ordinary and extraordinary beauty." A cool rainy day shifted the activity indoors, where we concentrated on exploring our environment using all the senses. We moved into a covered walkway outside and spread along it. With eyes closed, we focused on our other perceptions—smell, touch, and sound—and explored what was around us.

I leaned over to touch the rough-textured, raw wooden wall, damp from the rain, exuding an earthy pine smell. Just as I was about to move to another area, I felt a cold nose and wet head fill my hand. I opened my eyes to see a large German Shepherd dog staring up at me with her large, liquid amber eyes. I said, "Look at you. You're all wet." A warm sensation moved up my body. This was familiar territory. I put both hands on her head and started to gently stroke her from nose to ears. Her bright eyes and wet dog pungency filled the space as she relaxed and leaned against me.

DARCY
A Revelation

Then something strange happened. Tears welled up and my chest tightened with emotion. I knelt to be on her level. With one hand on her chest, the other went from wet nose to broad muscular head to soft ears, to the coarse hair on her thick neck. After a few minutes the retreat activity ended, and we moved out of the walkway and back into the hotel. She wanted to follow us in and I had to gently turn her around at the door. A final caress and she was gone.

I was in a daze walking back to our meeting room. Still shaken, unsettled, and confused by the wave of emotion the interaction unleashed. What just happened? Why did she come to me? I was near the front of our group, and she passed by several people in the walkway to get to me. During the debrief of our retreat activity, people spoke about how touched they were to see the compassion and tenderness of my interaction with the dog. Another wave of emotion rolled over me. I fought back tears.

At the time, I was a few months away from resuming my role as a clinician and teacher at the veterinary college I worked in. After ten years in administrative roles as a department chair and associate dean, I was returning to the teaching hospital as a small-animal internist. I had not planned to do this. That chapter of my life was closed, or so I thought. Budgetary cutbacks had eliminated my associate dean position four months prior. Years earlier, I had pursued academic administration because I was interested in leadership.

That was not the whole truth though. After being a busy academic clinician and teacher, I burned out. Maybe I had seen too much death and loss move through my patients, friends, and family. The thought of returning to clinical work filled me with anxiety and dread. *Did I belong there anymore? Was I still competent to practice? Could I euthanize another patient? Was the well of compassion still deep enough to hold the empathy and energy needed for me to be fully and wholly present to the work?* I wasn't sure and scared that it wasn't. The prospect of letting down my clients, patients, students, or colleagues haunted me.

I don't know what a revelation is, but this seemed like one. The physical and emotional experience stunned me. According to the *Stanford Encyclopedia of Philosophy*, "revelation" (or *revelatio* in Latin) is a translation of the Greek word, *apokalypsis*, which means "removal of the veil so that something can be seen." What did I need to see? Was it that animals were still part of me? That I still considered the bond between humans and animals a sacred and special thing? That I still was a caregiver? I took it as a cry from the darkness, telling me that I still had a role to play, a vocation to return to and to begin again as I had begun, using my head, hands, and heart as a veterinarian caring for animals. I was being called and welcomed home.

The episode gripped me in the days that followed and still does. I woke up well before dawn the next day, flicked on my bedside lamp, and in that small pool of light, sat in bed and wrote my first poem. I offer it here:

A GIFT

I lost you many years ago.
You settled below the surface with barely a ripple.
I didn't realize you had gone.
Other guides and lights took your place.

They lead me on other paths, rocky, uneven, unfamiliar.
I passed several mirrors along the way.
I was not sure who or what I was looking at.
You weren't there anymore. Where did you go?

It is said that when the student is ready the teacher
will arrive.
I didn't recognize you at first. You were soaked
with muddy feet.
But when I bent down and you laid your wet, warm
head in my hand,
there you were.

On a cold, rainy day in Chile, five thousand
miles from home,
a lovely dog brought my heart back to me.
Muchas gracias!

Darcy Shaw

PENNY
The Mystery of Gifts

Our lives interconnect in ways we can't know. Our simple acts may profoundly affect others. When Darcy met the German Shepherd dog and cradled its shaggy wet head in his hands, it touched every one of us. I can still recall the memory as if watching a movie—most powerfully, the love that shone between man and dog, all of us standing there in that passageway, rain pelting down just outside. I felt what it was to love unconditionally, to be loved without reserve. I remember one of the retreat participants saying, "I wanted to be that dog." And another, echoing, "We all did."

Now I realize another connection. I was excited to offer a retreat set in the lushness of the temperate rainforest of Chile. This was a new land for me. It felt important to begin our explorations of this place, and of ourselves in this place, using all of our senses. It would be more powerful to get out into the forest and breathe it in, touch it, smell it, hear it, see it up close than simply to observe it from our indoor meeting room. I had recently reawakened to the power of whole-body knowing and was alert to this rare opportunity.

The downpour on that morning called for a quick change of plans. In lieu of exploring out of doors, we moved the session into that fateful enclosed passageway, lined with windows and pungent from the rain—a fortuitous accident that opened our hearts as well as our senses.

A PROMPT HIDING IN PLAIN SIGHT?

Taking a step back, we wonder how our writing may invite your own explorations. Perhaps Darcy's poem "A Gift" will become your own prompt. Any of our stories may be a stimulus for your own writing, much as the poems or specific writing prompts we share. We invite you to be on the lookout for possibilities that tap into your own rich veins of memory.

CHAPTER SIX

What Keeps You Searching?

What maps do you use to navigate through the events of your life? Wayfinding can be challenging. Sometimes we follow a route that others have laid out only to discover as we go that we need to take other turns and follow different paths. Some signposts are obvious. You didn't get that job or position—now what? Other signs are more subtle, especially those lying just out of reach somewhere within us. Polynesian navigators traveled the Pacific Ocean by using stars but also birds, flotsam, wave patterns, and currents that suggested the presence of unseen land. That happens to us, too, when we feel the presence of something we need to do even though we can't see it yet. Our life may seem fine by all the usual measures, but there is a missing piece.

The writing in this chapter arose after struggling with prompts that initially didn't work for us. Some prompts failed to bring out writing that we liked. Others just didn't draw us in from the get-go. After reading the poem "Reporting Back to Queen Isabella" by Lorna Goodison, the prompt we gave ourselves was "write about an experience of abundance." The richness and lushness of newly discovered lands described in the poem led us there. However, we struck out with our online writing. It just fell flat to our own ears and hearts. Yet we didn't criticize or judge ourselves (or the poem!) but simply took it in stride. This topic of abundance didn't hit the mark. It could have, but it didn't.

Yet the conversation and reflections that followed gave rise to a powerful topic for both of us. We tried to imagine the role and expectations Don Cristobal had (the sailor-explorer in the poem) as he gathered plundered riches (even as he ignored the native people from whom he stole) to lay at the feet of Queen Isabella. This led us to consider the norm of doing what's expected. From there it was a natural step to wonder about what this implicit or explicit obligation meant for us. We had our prompt: "What role has doing what's expected played in your life?"

PENNY AT-HOME
What role has doing what's expected played in your life?

I'm not very good at doing what's expected. In fact, I would say I've had a long life of doing the unexpected in many ways and at many junctions.

Maybe by now what is expected is that I will do the unexpected. It feels like a miracle that I've carved my own path and doors opened at each turn (sometimes after other doors slammed shut) for me to create my professional life organically and in unexpected ways. I thought I wanted to be a field biologist (loving the outdoors and confusing my love of nature with a calling to make it my vocation). I got a doctorate in ecology and animal behavior, studying the foraging behavior of five species of woodland birds. That in itself was counter to expectation. My parents were artists and intellectuals. I was a city girl. Who could imagine it?

Halfway through I realized I was a people person and began to find my way into the rest of my life without ever getting a different degree. I learned by following my gut and heart and apprenticing myself to great teachers. I was legitimate in a way, but without certification—more by experience and chutzpah and a good deal of luck and support from people who took a chance on me.

In my long career I have been a therapist, a researcher of people's behavior as part of a city planning initiative, a group facilitator, a community psychologist, a teacher in medical education (helping students, residents, and faculty improve their communication skills, deepen self-awareness, realize that showing empathy and compassion are as important as technical skills, and more). I learned to teach leaders how to lead effectively and how to create healthy thriving organizations. I was a founding leader of three organizations in all these domains—wanting to pass along what was so hard-won for me.

I was mentored by great ones. George Engel taught me to listen. David Cooperrider taught me to look for what is working so as to do more of it. Parker Palmer taught me to discern and trust my inner teacher, to never stand outside the circle, and to create and lead Circles of Trust from that authentic place. Glenna Gerard taught me to listen to the flow of meaning moving through conversations. Others taught me to understand and hold group energy and flow. John Kabat-Zinn taught me to meditate. Arawana Hayashi opened me once again to the nuanced wisdom of the body within individuals and among collectives. Life taught me progressively to risk my vulnerability and heart again and again—to bring my true, imperfect, often scared, alive, loving self to all I did. Experiences sweet and sad, awful, funny, and informative filled in.

All those I worked with—partners, leaders, those I mentored or taught, all students of life—taught me the essential importance of relationships. I received and learned from each person; often far more than I felt I gave. I realized that being an empathic witness for others was a gift, and when I was destroyed by grief or fear, I finally let others be there for me in the same way I had tried to do for them.

I am not definable by degree or title or path, yet I have made a coherent life. I am true to myself, if not as well-versed or credentialed as I always thought I had to be to achieve legitimacy. I could write my life story as a series of successes. I could also tell it as a long line of missteps, failures, and new tries. I could easily share how much I love to be alive and to laugh—the laughter is how I know I'm on the right path. It is all true. So much has been unexpected, yet I am driven. What *is* in step with a defining mark of our culture has been my determination to succeed at much of what I set out to do. Nothing is 100 percent but I've had a damn good run—I still am!

DARCY AT-HOME
What role has doing what's expected played in your life?

I started crying in my fifties. Not randomly in public places, but in response to feelings that had been boxed up for decades. No longer was the container tight enough. Stuff began to seep out. A thick, sticky treacle that could not be wiped up and put back into its proper place.

Although doing what's expected has been a useful guide in many ways, like most things it has a dark side. For me, that darkness was the expectation that successful strong men didn't express emotion (except anger), at least the kind that led to tears. To be rational and in control was what was expected. I had a good role model for this in my father, who I never saw shed a tear. My mother was not far behind him. Anger, lots of anger, but not tears. As a child I considered feelings toxic, especially those that might result in crying and be interpreted as weakness or lack of control. The prospect of crying was way worse than sitting on poison ivy, falling off a roof, being grounded for a month, or cutting myself with a knife. Not for me. No way, Jose!

This, as it turned out, was a pretty successful strategy for educational and work-related advancement. I was the one who would not get ruffled in stressful situations. I did what I said I was going to do and was never the source of any drama. I really liked being the calm, collected, analytical one. This was conveniently reinforced by the media messaging around me. Movies and books provided limitless numbers of heroic and stoic male archetypes.

This all worked well, until it didn't. By my fifties I had been worn down by life's inevitable ups and downs. The ups were not a problem, but what to do with all the sorrow that had accumulated? Sorrow had filled the tailings pond that I built for it and was now threatening to burst its banks. I didn't have the resources or energy to shore it up, and deep down I knew that I shouldn't. There was a lake full of unfinished business, and its due date had arrived.

As chance or fate would have it, I found a way into the hard work of emotions. Participation in Courage & Renewal work and being held in a trusted safe space allowed me to venture into my emotional labyrinth. By then, it was more important to discover and honor who I was and had been rather than continue to live up to the unrealistic and distorted view of manhood. So I reflected, and was listened to. Tears were shed about the past, present, and future, and it was okay. Uncomfortable but okay. I came to see tears as a barometer of how open my heart and soul were and how ready I was to let the world and myself in. No longer the toxic enemy; just a visitor bringing a sense of healing and grace that could come from no other place.

So, in my fifties, my heart began to open and tears became my friend. In many ways my real life began then. I took longer than I thought to finally grow up, or at least realize that my heart and soul were important parts of me. I had relied on them in many ways as I discerned the right paths forward in my personal and professional lives, but had never acknowledged their presence. Ultimately, they became my savior. There is a Sioux proverb that states, "The longest journey a man will take in his life is from his head to his heart." So true, and such a long, rocky journey.

DISCOVERING THE QUESTION BENEATH THE QUESTION

A year later, when we reflected on our at-home writing about expectations, we wondered what further question was awaiting us. Our first attempt at a new prompt, "Where do I belong where

I can bring my whole self?" left us blank, which was a surprise. We got there after talking about expectations and roles and how sometimes they don't fit us. There is a need to belong and bring our whole selves to important endeavors, but there are times we can't. This is stuff we usually can sink our teeth into, but not this time, for whatever reason. After a false start, we landed on a prompt that was engaging for us both. We had discovered through our writing practice that there is often a rich question waiting to be asked beneath the first prompt. By staying curious, we uncovered a fruitful area for further exploration. Meaning-making comes in layers. We share our path and what emerged.

PENNY
Right Question, Wrong Framing?

It is notable how a question asked in one way can shut me down or leave me stymied about how to respond, whereas the same question asked differently unleashes memories, stories, thoughts, and feelings—and sometimes insights. That happened here. Our first prompt, "Where do I belong where I can bring my whole self?" left me stymied.

I struggled to tap into the rich vein I thought must be lurking just out of reach, but to no avail. It was as if the question already contained the punchline. There was no mystery, nowhere to go to discover new meaning.

Then I thought to frame the question differently. I asked myself, "What keeps me searching?" and the way opened. This feels like a useful lesson to highlight: if a question doesn't work for you, let it go and ask another one that opens the way. Trust that the kindling and logs of your fire are already there for the lighting. It takes the right match!

PENNY
What keeps me searching?

I have repeatedly sought to find my right place in the world where I can give what is mine to give, be seen and known for who I am, and feel that I am making even a small difference. The work and circumstances shifted as I grew and changed, was ready to move on from earlier endeavors, or delve more deeply in chosen directions, yet the underlying factors were the same.

What brings out my best? Work I believe in and that calls to me, a perceived need that I trust I can fill, an enticing challenge, a welcoming reception, and kindred partner(s). Being creative matters. I am drawn by the chance to strengthen relationships, travel to interesting locations, and engage in new collaborative opportunities.

Yet, while there is stretching that is life-giving, there is also searching that comes from a scarcity mindset. For many years, alongside the healthy motivations I describe above, lay the gnawing question: Am I meant to be great? Or the fear-driven wonderings: Am I in over my head? Am I giving all I can? Is there a better me, a bigger life to discover? Can I rest in who I am? These ego questions haunted me into my fifties and sixties. I was plagued by restlessness and anxiety as much as by the joy of the search until I made peace with who I am, found the work that both spoke to me and was the best fit, and learned to accept and even love all my parts (as I wrote about in chapter 4). Stretching to meet the next adventure while being present to the beauty and wonder of being alive right where I am is how I know my best self.

When I turned 70, I thought to myself, "I have paid my dues. From now on I will choose to do only what makes my heart sing." For me, that meant choices in all parts of life—the work I said yes to, the people I surrounded myself with, the love I opened to give and receive, the poignancy of life I let in through sadness, grief, fears, and uncertainties that come with having an open heart. My singing heart (I knew) had a range of music from exquisitely sad to joyfully happy; from quiet to boisterous. I was open to all of it, committed to live into each choice fully, whatever came. I knew that when I was exhausted from too much of everything, I couldn't really bring my best to anything or stop to reflect on what I was learning. The time had come to shift.

That moment marked the beginning of nuanced discernment and letting go. It meant saying a wholehearted yes only to "right work" and life-giving relationships. I recognized that I had agreed to a number of things that were just okay or that I had done for a long time but no longer lifted me. Now I felt the preciousness of time. I wanted islands of meaningful work and connections in a larger sea of spaciousness. For so many years I had said yes to everything (or so it seemed). My calendar was choked. That changed over the next several years as I made honest discernments about what most called to me at this time in my life. I said a wholehearted yes or no, guided by my heart's knowing.

Now, 11 years later, my aspiration is to bring all of myself to each day, whether I am coaching, leading a retreat, writing this book, taking a long walk, trying a new recipe, or having spacious time with a friend. I rejoice that the line between work and life has blurred! I know I am lucky.

Yet, as an elder, I am also aware of new challenges to this lifelong path.

Recently I experienced right leg pain severe enough to stop me from walking more than a block or two. I had to wait two weeks to be examined by a physician and get the tests that would shed light on diagnosis and treatment.

I had been walking four to five miles a day and this forced stopping of unknown cause and such frightening symptoms had a profound effect on me. I stopped feeling the daily aliveness and motivation that is so much a part of me. I stopped feeling like stretching, metaphorically. Fortunately, the vascular surgeon I saw diagnosed a treatable condition. He prescribed medication and a regimen of 30 minutes of daily walking in spite of the pain. It reframed my experience to know that walking through the pain was not only safe but helpful.

That same evening was chorus practice. I was leaning towards dropping out for the season, as I knew it would be a struggle to walk up the many stairs to the practice venue. I tentatively made my decision to stop this much-loved activity, feeling still the incapacity of the last few weeks.

Suddenly I felt my fighting spirit "kick in"—more like it kicked me awake. I had the clear thought, a message from my wiser self: "I've suffered a big loss these last two weeks. Hopefully I will get back to walking as before, but right now I can't. I don't need another big loss. I am not dead. I am not infirm. I'm going to chorus practice. I'm alive and intend to live fully for as long as I have."

And just like that, my inner sense of resilience and determination switched from "off" to "on." I was back once again, committed to living fully. It struck me that what keeps me searching is life itself.

DARCY
What keeps me searching?

What saves you some days is your writing partner! I too was laboring with the question about "belonging" and "whole self." Normally, these would be intriguing prompts to respond to, but it didn't resonate. It was with great relief that Penny wrote to me and said that after struggling with the at-home prompt, she'd found an opening—a new question and one that I found immediately compelling. "What keeps you searching?"

I'm sitting up in bed right now, with my wife Shelley sleeping beside me. It is early morning with the sky just beginning to brighten. We're in Halifax, Nova Scotia, for a funeral of a friend and colleague's father. I'm foggy, still recovering from a migraine yesterday. I went to bed early but was awake at 3:30 am. The question Penny posed is moving around my mind as I inhabit that liminal area between sleep and full awakeness. I'm looking at it from this angle and that. Holding it up and spinning it around like an interesting rock I picked up on a trail. Words and phrases are drifting by that are trying to find footing in response to the question.

What keeps me searching? What's the what? Is it that "I'm not finished yet" or is it curiosity, or is it the draw of mystery, or the anxious pull of uncertainty, or do I just want to understand how things work or how they'll turn out in the end?

Another related question is the focus of the search. Is this more about small, medium, or large things, or all of them as they arise over time, bidden and unbidden, surprising or not? I then remembered a recent search.

DARCY
Looking for Edges

I rolled out of bed a half an hour before my alarm went off. I couldn't sleep anymore, so I started my final preparations. The sun was just rising as I looked out our hotel window. We're perched high over the Ionian Sea in Taormina, Sicily. This is the day I've been waiting for. Over the last four months I've trained hard for this one objective.

I step out onto our balcony and turn to the south. There it is, partially draped in early morning mist that covers the lower reaches but leaves its snowcapped northside top exposed. Mount Etna is beautiful in the red light of a new day. Beautiful and intimidating because I'm climbing it today on my bicycle. It is Europe's most active volcano and erupted just a couple of months prior. It dominates the skyline of eastern Sicily.

I'll start my ride from a small coastal town about 10 minutes south of Taormina and climb up the eastern side of Etna. A little spasm of anxiety pierces my gut. That's familiar. I've felt it before other challenging rides. No matter how well you have prepared, you never know how you'll feel when you get to the hard stuff. How will my legs be today? Have I trained enough, both physically and mentally? My goal is to ride the two ascents it takes to get to the top nonstop. It will be an 80 km (50 mile) round trip, but the actual climb is 28 km (17.4 miles) that is split into two, 14-km (8.7 mile) segments. The first has an average gradient of 6% and the second climb sits at 6.5%. Not killer gradients, but this is a long climb by any standard in the road cycling world. I've never climbed this far and never a mountain this high. We'll get as high as 1740 meters (5709 feet) today when we reach Rifugio Citelli on the eastern slope of Etna before descending to the town of Linguaglossa and then back to where we started.

I laid out all of my cycling gear the night before: jersey, bib shorts, gloves, windbreaker, shoes, socks, helmet, sunglasses, pedals, head unit (bike computer), heart rate monitor, water bottles, snacks and energy gels, suntan lotion, lip moisturizer, cash, credit card, and cell phone. I check the weather forecast again to see if I need any extra layers. This is a ritual I enjoy. I have a predilection for process, or knowing exactly how something is going to happen from point A to B. I've spent hours thinking about all of the details and "what ifs" around this ride.

My taxi arrives to take me to the bike rental facility. I finish applying suntan lotion, pick up my bag of cycling gear, pause at the room door, and think if I've forgotten anything. I take a deep breath. I'm still feeling anxious about the day. There are many moving parts. Lots of things could go well and lots could go wrong. I've planned well; time to let go, it's game time.

I've booked a guide to take me up the mountain and learn when I get to the facility that there will be one more rider. He's Italian and about 10 years younger than me. He speaks no English, but I have a few words of Italian, so we share some stilted pleasantries. When our guide arrives, I get my bike and begin setting it up: pedals on, bike computer and speed sensor mounted, and seat height adjusted. The ride is going to be a long, hard effort and it's imperative that the bike is set up right so I'm comfortable and will not be distracted by unnecessary pain.

The Climb Begins

We're off. I fall in behind my riding partner and the guide as we wind our way out of town. We have about 6 km (3.7 miles) of gentle ups and downs through urban and suburban light industrial areas to reach the base of Mount Etna. My legs feel good so far. My anxiety eases as I settle into the rhythm of the ride and breathe deeply, enjoying the fresh early morning air as it fills my lungs and flows over my body.

At the base of the first climb we pause briefly as our guide lets us know what's ahead. We begin and I find a pace and effort that I know I can maintain. One of the things that surprised me about cycling is that it's important to train mentally as well. What's needed is a mindset that allows you to be comfortable (or at least accepting and open to) being very uncomfortable, sometimes for long periods of time. When every fiber of your being is screaming *stop, stop,* you say, "Yep, that's how it's supposed to feel and it's okay" and keep on pedaling.

The first climb took us through misty low cloud cover and into the partial sunlight. I am feeling good. We've climbed through farmland, vineyards, and small working towns. I managed the first climb well and am eager to continue. We stop briefly to rest and refuel. It's all about carbohydrates and energy. One burns calories at a prodigious rate during these efforts, and if you don't keep up you will, as cyclists say, bonk. This is when you've burned through all of your short-term energy reserves (glucose) in your muscles and liver, and become like a wet noodle, so weak you can hardly pedal.

We have about 5 to 6 km of rolling hills along a plateau before we reach our final ascent, which will be harder and higher. We again stop for a short time to drink and refuel, and up we go. Things feel good until about halfway up the last section. I can feel the accumulated effort heavy in my legs. From now on, it will be my mindset that will keep me pedaling. All my life I have had the ability to persevere during hard times. I put my head down and just keep going. This is good, but as the saying goes, "the flip side of a strength is often a weakness." The ability to grind it out has been good and also, at times, bad. It's kept me from making needed changes. On this day, however, I'll need an overflowing glass of it to get to the top.

The Final Push

We are 4 km from the top. My legs feel like lead weights and now the wind starts. We are nearing the treeline and a ferocious headwind assaults us. My guess is that it's gusting from 40 to 60 km/hr (25–37 mph) by the way I'm being buffeted on the bike. Cycling uphill is hard enough, but when it's into a headwind, it's downright demoralizing! I struggle on; my breathing is fast and deep but is becoming ragged.

At about 2.5 km from the top, we meet a small tour bus parked by the side of the road. It can't be. What are the odds? Shelley and some of our friends took a hiking tour on Mount Etna today while I did my cycling adventure. I never thought I would see them, but there they are. I recognize Shelley's bright pink windbreaker. As we near, I decide to stop despite my goal to keep going on the climbs. I need to. As I slow near the bus, my legs are trembling with fatigue. It's a mental boost to see them, and after a few minutes and some memorable photos, we forge on.

All I can think of is how many meters of road there are left to the top. The wind is battering us. I break the task down. Every 100 meters, I ask myself, *Can I go another 100? Yes, I can*—and keep going. I have to stop briefly one more time when a strong gust stops me in my tracks; I couldn't pedal through it. Just 1000 meters left. Some kind soul has painted the remaining distances every 100 meters on the side of the road. Nine hundred, 800, 700, and then at 300 meters we turn around a sharp hairpin and the wind is now behind us. Glory days! What a boost, literally. I can now see the Rifugio Citelli building and call up what little power is left in my legs. I stop in front of the building, slump forward over the handlebars, and carefully lift my wobbly leg over the saddle. The gusts are so strong here I am almost blown over. I stumble with my bike to the back of the building and out of the howling wind. Inside await some high-calorie snacks and one, probably two, espressos! A sense of relief and exhausted satisfaction rolls over me. It's done.

It's Not What It Seems

I searched for and found the edge of my physical and mental endurance. Maybe not the extreme edge, but I could sense it from where I was. Many would ask, "Why on earth would you put yourself through that?" A fair question that is not easily answered. I could flick off a superficial platitude like "Because it was there," or "I just wanted to test myself." There is of course some truth to that, but it goes deeper for me. Does it sound strange to say there is a spiritual element at play? After I come out of these intense, painful efforts that have taken me to ragged places, I'm a little changed. Extreme physical effort thrusts me into my body in a piercing and all-consuming way. Walt Whitman said that "If the body were not the soul, what is the soul?" I feel as if I bump into my soul during these hard exertions. Things around me look a bit different. I don't see myself as a victor that feels above and better, but as a humble (by being humbled!) human being that has been granted a truer glimpse of what is worthy and real in this world.

Our friend paradox is at play. By doing something that is so ego inflating, to test my physical limits and survive, the reverse seems to occur. Extreme suffering seems to sear away the preening, pouty ego to reveal something more elemental and compelling. It's right there hidden in plain sight inside us all. It's the pulsating radiant glow of our human spirit that does its work in the world through our hearts and souls. We all suffer. We all try to do our best. We all want to belong. We all want to know love. It's hard, but we do it anyway, again and again. We don't give up. I think that's what keeps me searching. Looking for, and hopefully touching, seeing, and being a part of that special soulful beauty that connects us all.

THE THREAD YOU FOLLOW

In William Stafford's wise poem "The Way It Is," he says, "There's a thread you follow. It goes among things that change. But it doesn't change . . . . You don't ever let go of the thread." We followed a thread through this chapter from question to question to question. Holding onto and following this thread was a way of navigating through the events of our lives sparked by the writing prompts. We held fast to the thread of our core selves, but where it was leading us was unknown. As questions begat questions, the thread led us to a richer and fuller understanding of who we were and how that happened.

This was meaning-making in action. We did not anticipate that in the process of writing this book, we would continue to peel back layers of meaning beyond where our original stories took us. It just keeps going. We can't seem to stop it. What a wonderful thing!

What else became apparent was how the poems seemed to unconsciously influence our writing even when we used prompts that diverged significantly from the poem's content. For example, in "Reporting Back to Queen Isabella," it talks about a journey, a lush island and mountains. Well darned if some of that imagery didn't show up in our writing and even in one of our prompts ("What keeps you searching?"). Things are working in us that we don't fathom. We get glimpses of them when we hit on the right prompt and stay open.

> There is in you something that waits and listens
> for the sound of the genuine in yourself . . .
> that is the only true guide you will ever have.
>
> **Howard Thurman**

CHAPTER SEVEN

The Shape of Beauty

For this writing session we read Yousif M. Qasmiyeh's poem "Writing the camp." It talked about living in a crowded, ever-changing refugee camp. We recognized that the poem's setting was outside of our lived personal experience, and as a result, we wrestled with it as a third thing. Still, we honored the truth of the poet's telling and were also impacted by the feelings, words, or phrases evoked. For example, when the camp's elderly midwife waits by the cemetery to intercept children on the way to school "to give them a kiss and remind them that she was the one who made them." We saw beauty here in the midst of much difficulty. As Ada Limón has said, "The poet's job is not to offer hope. The poet's job is to unleash feeling." It brought forth feelings of being in a crowded camp, watched by others, and of special human moments like the love and affection displayed by the midwife. These feelings and images worked in us as we approached our writing prompts.

We began to think about things that see us but we don't see. It gave rise to our online writing question, "What goes unnoticed that notices you?" Both of our responses to this talked about the people we don't see or only partially see but see us in ways that we can never truly and completely know. The writing that arose was okay but not engaging enough, at least to us, to include in this chapter. As noted in the previous chapter, sometimes, despite a good question, our writing didn't rise to the occasion. We just accepted that and moved on.

As we considered our at-home question for the week, we began to turn our initial question around. Something we found ourselves doing frequently. It started out as "What do we see but not notice?" It then evolved into "What is something you see but then see or connect to more deeply?" Inevitably, art came up as something we see and are impacted by, sometimes profoundly. At times, getting more specific with a question can be helpful. It provides more visible boundaries, which makes finding a way into the prompt easier and less overwhelming. We struggled with the right prompt, and remembered a recent *Poetry Unbound* newsletter by Pádraig Ó Tuama that had one which hit the right note (on only a few occasions did we use outside help in crafting prompts. Some days the best one just didn't come to us). Consequently, we settled on "When did art make something happen for you?" Now we had something we could get our teeth into. Both of us had ready examples of how art had moved us that we were eager to explore.

PENNY AT-HOME
When did art make something happen for you?

Discovering the art of Chiura Obata was a revelation. I was designing a retreat that I would lead in Japan, my first time in that country but not in my imagination. I had long felt an instinctive resonance with Japanese sensibilities— particularly the calligraphic art that captured mysteriously tall and magnificent mountains in clouds with a few ink brush strokes; or a flower or bird with remarkable economy of color and placement of object in space. (The classical question—"What is this?"—when shown a drawing of a curved "v" on an empty page is often met with "a bird flying" or "a 'v' in the air." The true answer is "a vast sky with a bird flying in it." Space is the most important element.)

I had settled on the theme of "beauty" for the retreat: what do we find beautiful? What is our experience of beauty? It seemed a perfect opportunity to reflect on cultural contexts of beauty along with each person's lived experience through Western or Japanese eyes.

I was well along in the planning when I happened to be in New York City for a day. I had gone to see the retrospective of Jasper Johns' wildly expressive abstract works at the then-new Whitney Museum. I walked along the High Line park, a marvel in itself with native plants, grasses, and the occasional sculpture on the elevated byway along the Hudson River. The Whitney is at the end—a wonderful gift to cap off the art-ramble. My day already felt complete. I didn't know what was just around the corner.

After enjoying the Jasper Johns pieces and the magnificent architecture of the new museum, with its spacious walls and windows on the river, I thought I'd visit a bit of the main collection. I went down one level and literally rounded the corner to find a small stunning woodcut of El Capitan. It was the same view made famous by Ansel Adams' photographs, yet in a distinctly Japanese style. The artist was new to me—Chiura Obata. I knew I had discovered a priceless treasure for my retreat. More than that, I had found a new way to explore beauty from a cultural context.

I love Ansel Adams' photographs of Yosemite and knew many of them intimately. For some years I had bought a wall calendar of his Yosemite photos and lived with his iconic images every month. Now I was struck by how the same natural beauty could be so familiar yet so different when rendered through Japanese sensibilities. When I returned home, I researched Obata and discovered to my delight that he too was captivated by Yosemite. He had made many woodcuts of the same views that Ansel Adams captured with his photographs.

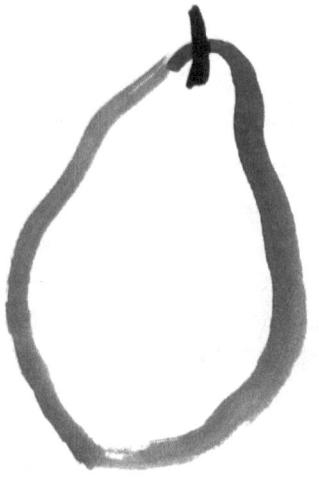

a red pear
full of sweetness
luscious anticipation

I copied prints of three views by each artist and used these to invite exploration and reflection.

Obata's woodcuts found a home in my heart. In Japan, we stayed at a rural retreat site with views of the Japanese Alps and Mt. Fuji. I felt I was seeing Obata come to life. It was like my first experience in Paris and the French countryside with the light and scenes reflected in Impressionist paintings capturing reality—art and life intertwined.

The striking difference was that Chiura Obata brought his sensibilities with him to the American West. In Japan, mountains look "Japanese" to my eyes. In France, the light and views resemble the French Impressionist paintings. In Yosemite, the eyes of the artist conferred their differences in rendering beauty. I held the question (probably without knowing it), "What is the shape of beauty that resides in me?"

Fast forward to 2021—only five years, yet a lifetime later. When the pandemic came in 2020, I experienced a year and more of imposed-yet-welcome solitude, stillness, and spaciousness. It is still a mystery to me what emerged. I wonder if the part of me that resonates harmonically with Japan found a way to emerge. Over a several-month period, I created a series of simple drawings with calligraphy ink and a small brush— some in black, some with colors. I called them "essence drawings," as I felt I captured something core to each form with just a line or two. Each drawing gave rise to a few lines of poetry—like a haiku, yet not pure-form.

They felt "right" to me, even beautiful. I loved them. The art of Chiura Obata was the catalyst. As unexpectedly as that wellspring of expression opened, it then closed and has not returned. I am not questioning it. It simply happened. I am grateful.

DARCY AT-HOME
When did art make something happen for you?

My wife Shelley and I were in the Moose Jaw Art Museum and Gallery. It's a small, unpretentious place connected to the public library and nestled into the banks of Crescent Park's creek. A cherished stop when home visiting my parents. On this day, my mom was with us and we were there to see an exhibition by local artist Gus Froese. Gus had been a long-time family friend. He lived just up the street from where I grew up and I played with his kids. Gus was also my grade-nine art teacher.

I was in my early forties and a lot had happened over the preceding few years. My father had recently passed away, as well as a close friend. It had become clear that Shelley and I were not going to be parents. I'd been a clinician in a busy academic post for close to 20 years and was burning out. My term as president and a council member of the Canadian Veterinary Medical Association had just ended after eight busy and thrilling years. A lot of change and loss. I felt untethered and at the edge of an abyss. To paraphrase Dante at the beginning of his *Divine Comedy*, in midlife I found myself in dark woods, the right road lost. I had lost hold of who I was, what I was supposed to do next, and where I belonged. All this to set the stage for how and what I encountered looking at a retrospective of Gus's work.

Gus was born in Saskatchewan and lived his whole life on the prairies. It's no surprise that this is what he painted. What caught my attention was a linear series of five, one-foot-square panels depicting a traditional orange grain elevator, luminous against a dark background of approaching thunderclouds. The panels depicted the storm's steady march towards the elevator. I had experienced this weather many times while growing up. I could feel the still, humid air, scents of dry grass and sage lingering in the electrified quiet before the storm. Low rumbling in the distance felt in your feet and rolling over your skin. A storm was coming. How bad would it be? How violent? How long?

This pentaptych of a prairie summer storm offered me a handhold and a metaphorical warning of the dark years ahead. A storm was coming, black clouds loomed. The pictures connected me to the prairie landscape where I grew up. To the dark soil, oceans of grass, golden wheat fields, and endless sky. To the toils of my grandparents who farmed this land. To my family and relatives and to those who had moved through this land for millennia. It rekindled my love of the prairie and its windblown, dusty grassland beauty. It was rooted inside me, and I'd forgotten about it. This was something I could hold on to as storm clouds gathered. I can see this now, looking back. It was not obvious to me at the time.

We bumped into Gus a few days later when visiting a small town near Moose Jaw. I needed a tangible piece of the prairies to take back to Prince Edward Island. Gus was thrilled to reconnect and invited us over to his studio. Although the storm series was not available, a painting of the North Saskatchewan River in fall colors was a good substitute. It hangs over the bed in our guest bedroom.

I wrote to Gus after the picture had been shipped and delivered. I said that the prairies give up their beauty reluctantly. You must be there for a while, to sit, listen, breathe in its spirit, and see what emerges. You need to meet it on its own terms. Gus loved that. We never spoke again. Fifteen years later in the spring of 2017, Gus passed away. He had given me something to hold on to when I needed it. I wish I could have thanked him for that. He thought he gave me a painting, but what he really gave me was an anchor to keep me from being swept away in the spiritual storm that was beginning.

THE BEAUTY OF BEAUTY

Like previous chapters, as we came back and read through our earlier at-home writing, it led to more conversation about the images, themes, or words that came up in what we wrote. The exploration of art, not surprisingly, prompted a discussion on beauty. An attractive (no pun intended) topic that has many layers and angles. We recognized that what we think is beautiful, and why and how it pulls us forward, is lodged firmly inside each one of us. The shape of it is unique to each person's experience and their singular history, struggles, dreams, and hopes. We began to wonder if the universal felt experience of beauty impacts us more than just the in-the-moment gasps when we experience it. Does it influence our lives and the decisions we make in significant and unseen ways? We wanted to plumb that thought further, which led to the writing prompt, "How has beauty been a wayfinder for you?"

PENNY
How has beauty been a wayfinder for you?

Beauty matters to me. More than that, it is life-giving. It is an organizing principle for me. I don't believe I could live without beauty—beauty in nature, beauty in human-made form, inner beauty. I have shared elsewhere in these pages my love of art, music, and movement. Now I find myself drawn to write about the seminal place in my life of nature's beauty.

There is a longing in my soul that can only be filled by the exquisite, ever-changing beauty of the natural world. The earth's beauty has always had the power to sing to my heart, lift my spirit, settle my being. It has informed my choices, large and small, at every juncture.

For seven years I was fortunate to live on Bainbridge Island, in Seattle, Washington, and commute by ferry the nine miles across Puget Sound to the university where I taught. I never, not for a day, took it for granted the magnificence of the Cascade and Olympic Mountain ranges, the iconic Mt. Rainier, the shifting colors and moods of the water, the accessible coniferous forests with myriad hiking trails. I called it my soul home, and it was true. I belonged there and I knew it.

Yet I left. I left for reasons of necessity and competing tugs on my heart. When my daughter Jessica was 14, she decided to move back East to live with her father, who made her an all-or-nothing offer—to live with him full time or not see him at all. She hadn't seen him for even a visit in the prior 18 months and felt compelled to go.

When Jessie left, even the mountains were not enough to soften the gaping ache in my heart. In that first winter of her absence, I struggled to find my way. The beauty of flowers saved me. Each Saturday morning, I made my way to the iconic Pike Place Market on the Seattle waterfront and brought home an enormous bouquet of flowers, farmed and sold by the local community of Cambodian immigrants and brought to market. The flowers boasted a profusion of colors and types, the massive arrangements wrapped in cones of paper bound with ribbon.

There were enough flowers in one bouquet for me to place them everywhere in my home—six vases of beauty. Wherever my eyes lighted, I saw loveliness. I can still conjure the image of sitting in my living room, seeing the deep purples and pinks of a small jar of anemones with their jet-black centers. I can still feel how the unbearable weight of loss was eased a little each time.

Not too long after, I moved back East. I knew Jessie needed me nearby, and I needed to be closer to her. Being her mother was more of a pull than staying in that beloved place. At the time I was certain I would one day move back to the Pacific Northwest. The land, the water, the mountains, and my community of friends all called to me. Yet, it didn't happen. I fell in love with and married Jim, my longtime friend and one-time boyfriend. Jim was solidly ensconced in Baltimore; his life of writing and community was centered in that city. When Jim said he would move to the Northwest with me if that was the only place I could find a job, he added, "It will probably kill me." I knew I couldn't do that. I loved him more than I loved the beloved geography.

That discernment led in large part to my decision to create a peripatetic life. If I couldn't live in the place of natural beauty that most called my heart, I would find ways to bring my work to settings that allowed me to spend regular time close to water or mountains. For many years I traveled often to lead workshops, retreats, and other programs in addition to my local work. Baltimore was home, and the world was home—I tuned in to the beauty of each place, adding time whenever possible to explore the particularities of season and land wherever I was.

In Baltimore, Jim and I moved into a small Victorian home with a large side lot just waiting for the right vision. With the help of my dear and talented friend Jeff, a landscape gardener and tireless creator of beauty, we laid out an English garden with a graceful path lined with hostas, flowering rhododendron, and spirea bushes, and planted a small Japanese maple that grew to tower gracefully over a round teak table and four chairs, the focal point of my backyard haven. And every week I still made sure that cut flowers graced our home in places the eye might rest. I had found my way.

DARCY
How has beauty been a wayfinder for you?

The Mote in a Cat's Eye

Have you ever looked into a cat's eye? I mean really looked, been absorbed by it, and almost fallen into what beckons—mystery, rapture, sanctuary? I have and fell completely in. I'm still falling and never want to save myself. What else could I do after gazing deeply at the green-yellow-gold, iridescent iris nestled in the eye of a black cat? Beholding two luminous moons set in a midnight face. You can forget to breathe looking at these improbable living jewels that are gazing at you. As you ponder them, they ponder you.

I adore cats! I'm continually fascinated and in awe of them. For me, they glow with all that's right in the animal world. And yes, they are beautiful to look at in all their shapes, colors, and sizes, as well as to touch. Just to feel their powerful, lithe muscles moving under your hands and sense the rippling energy pent up in their wild hearts wakes you up to your own aliveness.

John O'Donohue, the much-loved Irish poet and philosopher, said that "Beauty is that in the presence of which we feel more alive." I would add that for me, it also opens your heart.

Beauty does this time and again. I've come to realize that anything that opens my heart inevitably opens my soul. It starts a conversation within me about wholeness. A sense that in the presence of beauty, somehow everything is right with the world, it's okay to be hopeful, and somewhere, somehow, there is a place for me in it.

A North Star

I didn't know at 10 years old that I wanted to be a veterinarian. Many applicants to veterinary school report this, but not me. I came to it gradually, circling around the idea through my teenage years and into my first year of university. Then I decided and was all in. Looking back, this was mostly because it felt right. Yes, I could come up with any number of practical reasons, like it's a respected profession, the pay is okay, and I'd never be without a job. Yet I didn't listen closely to that voice. Rather, it just felt right deep inside me, that somehow it fit and I belonged there.

There is a surprising and radical question that has never occurred to me. Did beauty guide me into the veterinary profession? Was it the channel I was tuned into when thinking it just felt right? I can see the connections. If I was going to commit my life to a vocation, I wanted it to be meaningful work that engaged my head and heart. My heart was the deciding factor. I was looking for something to open my heart, and beauty does that. Granted, many animals are stunningly beautiful, sometimes ridiculously so. Can anyone explain a male peacock's extravagant, over-the-top plumage? It's like nature had a slow day and said, "Hmm. I heard someone wanted a prettier bird and I have a few spare parts laying about. Let's see what I can do."

For me, however, it's the spiritual beauty of animals that really takes my breath away. Their hearts and souls capture mine. The real beauty is the inherent wholeness that radiates from them. They don't spend their lives trying to be something they are not. They are who they are, with no apologies or qualifications attached or needed. They live fully in the moment. That is why animals are so compelling. They show us the way into our own wholeness and integrity. Something I desperately needed as a 19-year-old university student struggling with who I was and what I should do with my life. I feel more complete in the presence of animals. They round me out, smooth my edges, and open me to compassion. They take me out of myself and into something larger and life giving. I've journeyed a lifetime trying to find and live into my wholeness, and animals have always been trusted guides and cherished traveling companions.

Coming Back Home

Beauty has pulled me into other places too. When I find myself swallowed up by the grass- and sage-filled prairies, standing in awe amidst giant sequoia trees, or moving slowly through a deafeningly quiet, honey-colored slot canyon, my heart opens. I find completeness and connection there too. Borders are getting blurred between subjective feeling and the objective knowing of the world around us. A "poetic" ecology is emerging where the subjective feeling and response of organisms in ecosystems forms an integral part of how the system operates and survives. Andreas Weber suggests that our experience of felt beauty may be one of the most reliable indicators of healthy ecosystems.[5] So, beauty may be a barometer of what's right in the natural world. Could beauty be a pervasive organizing principle, an unrecognized central law of the universe (more vital than even the Higgs boson!), embedded in the Big Bang and dispersed everywhere like stardust? One can only hope.

I think beauty may be having a moment. Science seems to be affirming what we already knew in our sinews and bones. We evolved in nature with the scents, sounds, and sights of rivers, trees, mountains, and deserts flowing through us. We started

---

5 Andreas Weber, *The Biology of Wonder: Aliveness, Feeling and the Metamorphosis of Science.* New Society Publishers, 2016.

out whole like everything else and still are. When we are back in nature, we are reminded of that. Beauty connects us to the unseen river that runs beneath and through all things, cleansing, collecting, and welcoming us all home.

Look into the eye of a cat or any animal, kneel down and thrust your hand into the soil that birthed everything, smell the air that has bathed us for countless millennia. It just feels right and it's beautiful.

ENDNOTE

Considering our reflections here, we are struck by the centrality of beauty as an organizing force in our lives. We have different life experiences, have made different life choices, and see the world through different lenses. Yet we come to common ground. We have listened to our heart's knowing and we have each found our soul's home, again and again. Beauty has been a solace, a teacher, a compass, and a trustworthy friend. Broadly defined, beauty has helped each of us discover "right relation" within ourselves and in the world. It is a lifetime journey.

As with many of our writing prompts, we have different ways "in." With delight, we discover in these glimpses that each of our ways is a viable tributary into the universal sea of belonging and life.

Let the beauty we love be what we do.
There are hundreds of ways to kneel and kiss the ground.

Rumi

CHAPTER EIGHT

Belonging

In the previous chapter we talked about how beauty helped us find the right relation to ourselves and to the world. This chapter explores another facet of relation—the need, sometimes aching, to belong and the untethered paradox of not belonging. In Jónína Kirton's poem "reconciliation," she begins with "how will I reconcile myself? / the Icelander and the Metís / the settler and the Indigenous . . ." It made us talk about where we belonged or didn't belong and how that influenced our lives. The emotional tension of not belonging and the paradox of this as a potential gift grabbed our attention. For our at-home writing, we settled on, "How has 'not belonging' been a gift or strength for you?"

Being a bridge featured prominently in the poem and although we framed a question about it ("What worlds have you bridged?") for our online writing, the result didn't move us, so we did not include it here. As has happened in previous chapters, the online writing sometimes seemed to be a warm-up for our much richer at-home writing. Our process may contribute to this, as we used a time limit of 10 to 15 (maybe 20) minutes for our online writing versus no time limit for at-home work. That and coming to the online session not always fresh and rested may have led to less inspired prose. Regardless, we carried on.

The siren song of belonging echoes through the latter part of the chapter, where we reflect on how friendship has ushered us into the deeper waters of self-knowledge and exposed the generative and elemental interplay of love and connection.

PENNY AT-HOME
How has "not belonging" been a gift or strength for you?

"Not belonging" defines me in many ways—some unasked for, some chosen. My parents were Jewish but not religious. They made fun of religion, yet cared about all things Jewish in an ethnic sense—food, humor, and identity at the top. It made me a "non-belonger" among my grade school and high school classmates, all of whom went to church or (for the few Jewish kids) to synagogue, and the weekend religious schools and camps that created communities I didn't even know about until much later.

In the reactionary way of humans (at least this one), Mama and Papa's eschewing religion made me curious to learn about others' beliefs. Even though for some years I inwardly adopted the skeptical attitude of my parents, I also envied parts of what I glimpsed as easy belonging.

When I was 10, we moved from New York City to a working class, blue-collar suburb 20 miles north. I didn't belong in a new way. I was college-bound from birth and couldn't imagine anything else. I loved serious conversations about life and meaning and felt alone in that love. These conferred differences threw me on my own resources. I decided to try everything and be as good as I could be (an innate competitiveness in a town where ambition for school learning was not high). I could pursue and achieve what I wished in that reality. I became an editor of my high school yearbook, got a lead in our senior play, and made good grades. I propelled myself out of that town with a scholarship and loan to college. I was often lonely but driven and thankfully had an innate happiness and excitement. I knew there must be the possibility of connections that had eluded me thus far and was determined to find them.

The gift of those early years was to create a career and a life of making and fostering authentic relationships. I seemed to have radar for others' loneliness and feelings of being set apart. It took me a long time to learn that almost everyone feels they "don't belong" in some way. Being an outsider, I liked to listen from early on and occasionally would find a way "in" with unlikely school mates. When I was a young teenager, word got out that I knew about sex (not from any experience at all, but from my Bohemian liberal parents who felt it important to teach me about everything, and I mean everything). I became a go-to source of information for a few girls and hope I prevented some early pregnancies, since my mom also taught me about contraceptives! Those girls and I were never close, though.

In college, I found I was comfortable with lots of people when I asked them about themselves and listened to their stories. People confided in me. I am grateful I found my way to being a bridge for others to open up, to share, to feel less alone, to connect with others. Helping others to feel heard was a gift that resulted from my early life experiences of not belonging and I am grateful now for all of it.

Ultimately, I found that I needed to reveal more of myself and risk sharing my own vulnerability and feelings if I was to find a true sense of belonging and not just being there as a holder of others' stories.

A particular event comes to mind. For many years I led a weekly reflection group for primary care physicians, focused on their experience of being doctors (as part of a longitudinal faculty development program at Johns Hopkins Bayview Medical Center). As trust grew in each year-long group, the sharing was often intimate and poignant. Participants told of mistakes they had made, doubts or fears, struggles and exhaustion, funny moments, hard personal challenges, and more.

Early in one such year (not long after I moved from Seattle back to Baltimore), my teenage daughter had become an inpatient in a psychiatric hospital, having been diagnosed with bipolar illness after months of erratic behavior. It was a frightening and unknown time for me and yet I had kept my personal struggles private, never saying a word about my situation during group sessions. After those meetings with so many emotions often dredged up, I would sometimes cry alone in my office, overcome with angst yet feeling it would be unprofessional to share any of it. After all, I was the leader of the group.

One day about halfway through the year, one of the group members, a likable young physician I'll call Joe, casually mentioned that he had a patient who was crazy. He said it in a dismissive, even derisive tone. A few minutes later, he said that she was bipolar. That offhand remark cracked me open. I felt if I did not speak, I would not be able to live with myself. Listening to Joe toss off a derogatory label, I felt scared for what my daughter might face when back in the real world. I had experienced Joe as a caring person. If he could so easily dismiss a patient as crazy, how would he and other providers see beyond the label to the beautiful, struggling human person Jessie was? How would she fare?

I took a deep breath and said: "I have to tell you something. During this year, I have experienced how compassionate and thoughtful you are. It makes me intensely sad and afraid to hear you call one of your patients 'crazy.' My 15-year-old daughter is in a psychiatric hospital learning to navigate her way with bipolar illness. I know what a courageous, beautiful human being she is, and I'm scared she will not be seen behind the label when she is living in the world, particularly by physicians from whom she'll need support."

I choked up when I spoke. I was fearful of the response. He looked at me, and also with emotion in his voice, said, "I am so glad you told me. I don't think I will ever say something like that again. You just helped me see my patient as a person."

That was a revelation. I felt changed by daring to speak up on behalf of someone who mattered more than anyone in the world to me. In speaking my own truth, I realized that I became an ally for my daughter and a compassionate teacher for that physician and for the group. I also became more human to the group. I was neither discounted nor disrespected.

What helped me turn that fateful corner was the relationships I had built with Joe and other members of the group. I claimed my own voice and was held even as I held others. I could most easily defend someone I loved, which was the start. Over time, I came to realize that being a leader didn't necessitate standing outside of an experience. In fact, it gave me a special opportunity. When I showed vulnerability as a leader, it helped others show up. The vulnerability and courage of others helped open me to share in return. The mutuality of sharing in the welcoming, nonjudgmental spaces that I helped create became the bridge that I could trust myself on and opened pathways for finding true community and, finally, for experiencing a sense of belonging.

DARCY AT-HOME
How has "not belonging" been a gift or strength for you?

I've always been okay with not belonging. Not with being ostracized intentionally, but comfortable being along the edges or just outside the circle. It provides the clearest view of the landscape and ongoing or impending action (or threats). Maybe this comes from my introverted tendency that orients me to internal rather than external dialogue. Perhaps it's a reflection of my preference for independence. Who knows. What is evident is that I've intentionally stepped into not belonging. An example is the distance I've put between myself and religion. It was not a violent rupture but a gradual buildup of small things that led me as a teenager to conclude that religion just didn't make sense. Not only were the factual claims more than a bit sketchy, the church, at least my Roman Catholic one, had a long and troubled history of being a prime instigator of much bloodshed, suffering, and political intrigue. Mix that in with a misogynistic orientation and a top-down hierarchical structure that dictated what I was to believe and how I should live my life, and well, that seemed a bit much and more than a tad hypocritical. I wasn't having it.

Although these thoughts crystallized more coherently in my teenage years, even as a child I resisted being summarily told what to do. I remember the first time I made a priest mad. I went to a Catholic grade school and in preparing for my first communion, I was to take several sheets of information on the event home to my parents. I somehow forgot to do that and when I had a sit-down meeting with the priest a few days before the event, he asked if I had shared the documents with my parents and told them the time and date. I was up front and honest (as a politically naive seven-year-old can be) and told him I forgot in a nonchalant, visibly unconcerned manner. Then he got angry. I was surprised, as I had never seen a priest be more than distantly polite. I remember thinking that it was kind of interesting. Maybe that was the first time I began to wonder about the validity of the church. I subsequently went through my first communion and then later, confirmation, but never felt I belonged or had much in common with the institution.

The gift was the opportunity to see the world through many lenses, not just through those approved by religion. It was up to me to decide what was right or wrong, black or white, or just plain gray. It softened my edges and, in many cases, blurred them to nonrecognition. It wasn't me versus you or my tribe versus your tribe. It was us. The whole darn lot of us with all of our differences, but simply differences to be seen and valued. Most of us are just doing our best to live our lives with some dignity and purpose. No need for righteous condemnation or othering if we are not on the straight and narrow or not following "the way," whatever that may be.

That's not to say that belonging to a group or community can't help and support us through tough times. The decision to make is: what do you want to belong to and how? Which groups or communities are life-giving and welcome all of who you are, act with compassion, and allow space for you to struggle and evolve? When I find these groups, I sit in the circle, open my heart, and smile.

THE PILGRIMAGE TO FRIENDSHIP AND BELONGING

As we reflected on the arc of our journeys, we recognized that each of us had found our way to choiceful belonging. Belonging seemed inextricably linked to friendships, to finding kindred spirits with whom to travel. We were drawn to explore the connections and gave ourselves the writing prompt "What has friendship awakened in you?" On looking back at what we wrote, we recognized that friendships had been the path to belonging. Telling our stories of important friendships over time and at poignant moments in time made more visible the pilgrimage we had each been on. We retitled this section to name what our writing had uncovered.

PENNY
Celebrating Friendship

Having dear friends and knowing that I am a beloved friend has been a lifeline for many years. Not always. It took me a long time to learn to be a good friend.

Some months before I turned 50, I was talking with my close friend Roz who asked how I wanted to celebrate this momentous occasion. (Roz lived in a different city. We saw each other several times a year when our work brought us together and kept in touch by phone between meetings. We had each known tragedy and joys and now shared easily and deeply when we met.) On this day we were walking on Embassy Row in Washington, DC. It was a sunny spring day. I remember the blue sky and the blossoming cherry trees, the lightness of the air, the magnificent mansions, each the diplomatic headquarters for a different country. I remember saying, "The most important thing to me is the people I love and the people who love me. That is what I want to celebrate."

Right then and there I had the idea to host a weekend party so that far-flung friends might come for an evening and a day, joined by those who lived locally. It was an outlandishly extravagant plan, and it was absolutely perfect! Wanting to celebrate friendship rather than, say, going on a trip to Europe, was a testament to what mattered to me. My friends awakened my desire to give back. I felt joyful, grateful, mindful of our many shared experiences, and eager to bring together old friends as well as introducing people I loved to each other.

I was able to reserve the spacious colonial Georgian mansion in which I was then holding seasonal retreats. It was a beautiful location set in rural Maryland on 68 acres of bucolic countryside. The home had bedrooms for 26 people and could easily accommodate a gathering of 50. I didn't have a lot of money and asked my out-of-town friends to contribute to the cost of their accommodations. To my delight, they gladly agreed. That made it possible for me to make it happen: hire a DJ, arrange for the sumptuous food I so appreciated (Southern fare at its best) for the party and dinner on the first evening and breakfast the following day.

My friends came from many parts of my life. I wanted to share the bounty that friendship brings in a relaxed, celebratory way, with time for sitting and talking in the little nooks and crannies of that lovely mansion, walking in the outdoor beauty, as well as the dinner and dancing that made it a festive party. This was not my usual experience—it was my waking dream made manifest.

At dinner I told everyone I was celebrating them—friends I loved who also loved me. We all felt so happy and alive, still young yet on the cusp of the next chapter.

Friendship comes most easily to me one on one, or as part of a small group, over a long time. That party was the culmination of countless moments of sharing our lives.

Friendship has taught me to receive love as well as to give it, to let others help me as well as being there for them. I had to discover that lesson in my work life and I learned it again in my friendships. For many years I didn't know I was worthy of the love of friends. It was easy for me to give—to be the holder of others' secrets and stories, to listen, to share laughter and tears. I didn't fully believe that my friends would also want to have my back, would go out of their way to help me in my own time of need. That was in large part because I kept my own needs private, rarely sharing struggles that plagued me. Until I couldn't. Thank goodness.

PENNY
Friendships Through Hard Times

When my dear Jim was diagnosed with an incurable illness, I learned new truths about the immense steadfastness of friendship. Above all, Jim's love and friendship were remarkable. He was a fiercely independent and private man. He had never been sick, ever. Then he was very sick. His most loving gift was to let me in, to let me help care for him, to be his ally and sometimes his voice with his medical team, and to trust that I would guard his independence as best I could. He turned to me in a way he never had to before, to bring him to countless medical appointments, for counsel about his work commitments, and for taking over myriad household matters. We were each other's best friends and made our way through those hard six months with a sweetness and love that touched my very soul.

I canceled my work trips. I felt honored to care for him. He did all he could to stave off the illness while finishing the book he was writing.[6] He never complained. On one warm spring day when Jim was already too weak to walk, we took a long drive in the Maryland countryside in my little Mini convertible with the top down. It was an area we had hiked in for over 30 years. Now we found pleasure in the drive. It was a gift to me that Jim accepted my invitation to pause in his writing to go on that ride. I will never forget that day.

---

6 Jim completed his book *The World the Trains Made: A Century of Great Railroad Architecture in the United States and Canada* and saw the final proofs shortly before he died. It was published posthumously.

That was a private time of hunkering down. The two of us became the world. Dear friends were there for phone calls where I could sometimes admit my fear and let tears come. The outside hope was that Jim might still have five years. But it was not to be.

When he died, friends were beautifully there for me in new ways. They had respected our need for privacy. Now they showed up to hold me and help me in countless acts of kindness I couldn't have imagined. My immensely generous friend Sue came to the intensive care unit to be with me the night Jim died. She left a conference she was helping to lead when I called to say he may not make it. I was scared and alone, and she came, and she stayed.

The hardest hours after Jim died were at dinner time. It had been our best part of the day, eating good food and talking and laughing. Without ever discussing it, my daughter Jessie and her husband Steve were always available when I called each day at 6 pm. They kept me company during that hour. They knew me, they "got me," and they did this without fanfare for many months. Friends called, they wrote loving cards, they sent little messages, they offered help, and they meant it.

Six weeks after Jim died, my dear friends Wendy and Lynn traveled from their respective cities to help me organize and plan how to clear our home of 35 years of Jim's books and papers (as a writer he had almost never met a piece of paper or a book that he could part with) and how to reconfigure my living space for one person. It was an overwhelming task, and I was paralyzed by grief and the mountains of stuff. Their practical help, their comfort, and their presence were lifesaving. I felt held and loved. I glimpsed a way forward, emotionally and practically.

I had always felt competent to handle my life on my own. In fact, I thought I had to. I truly didn't know others would have my back in the countless ways that happened then. I was immensely grateful and vowed to myself to be there for others the way so many dear friends were there for me.

PENNY
Friendships as a Lifeline

My friendships have helped me believe I am good company, a person worthy of love. I love my friends. They love me. I know it in my bones. At times I've wondered why someone so (you name it) young, accomplished, creative, wise, etc., would want me as their friend. Ultimately, I've just accepted the truth of it.

We've been there for each other, listened to our daily musings, our times of despair or exultation. We have shared hopes, dreams, confusions, plans, failures, and delights. We have laughed together (oh how we've laughed) and held each other with compassion when tears came. It is the greatest solace for me to share tears with another. We have listened and been listened to.

A few friends have broken my heart, betrayed my trust. Those were hard lessons. Yet they taught me to be more clear-eyed, attentive to my own well-being. I am grateful I did not close down to the possibility of trust and love. Painful as those times were, I found solace in believing in my own self-worth. I did not betray myself.

Friendship is a close cousin to loss. In his powerful book *The Wild Edge of Sorrow*, Francis Weller reminds us that "everything you love you will lose." Having a friend means being willing to hold that reality. Dear friends have moved away, or I have moved and lost the easy chances to be in the kind of regular touch that is so nurturing. Others have become gravely ill and some have died. I have learned that such losses always feel unbearable and yet I can bear them. I want to bear them. Bearing loss is part of the whole.

It is all the little acts of friendship that matter. Ultimately those moments, days, and years add up to sharing life journeys with another for however long we have. It means being accepted and loved for who we are, quirks and all, and doing the same for our friends.

Friendships are my lifeline. They have made me a better person in all ways. For all of it, I am grateful.

DARCY
Losing a Friend

Yesterday I went to the hospital to say goodbye to a friend. Not the best place to say goodbyes because in that place, it's usually final. No "See you later," "Take care," or "All the best." It was the last time I'll see, hear, or touch him and share whatever words I could muster.

He is dying of ALS (amyotrophic lateral sclerosis) and has been lying in ICU on a ventilator for the last few weeks. Although he had been failing and getting weaker for many months, it was only after an episode where his wife found him unresponsive at home due to respiratory failure that the diagnosis became clear. ALS is one of the crueler diseases as it gradually robs a person of their muscle strength. When it advances to involve the respiratory muscles that keep you breathing, that is the end. The only reason my friend is still alive is that he is on a ventilator that is largely doing the breathing for him.

When Shelley and I walked into his ICU room, his wife was there, who is also a longtime friend of ours. Nestled comfortably on my friend's legs was their tabby cat, brought in for a special visit, and who we were going to take back to their home after the visit. I looked at him and was pleasantly surprised to see some light in his eyes. The last time he was heavily sedated because he was intubated.

Their beautiful and very relaxed cat was a comforting focal point for our initial conversation that drew us all to common and welcoming ground. We all loved cats, and as animals often do, it opened our hearts to fully inhabit this special time and place.

Both Shelley and I had thought about our final words. It's always hard to know what the right ones are. What made it particularly poignant was that we knew within a day or so when our friend was going to die. You see, he had made a decision to end his life through the use of the MAID program (Medical Assistance in Dying) that is available and legal in all provinces in Canada. He was going to be moved home and the procedure done there within the next week. As veterinarians, both Shelley and I have lots of experience with planned end-of-life events, but this was the first time it had involved a human being, and a friend. The premeditation of it was both familiar and unfamiliar.

My friend was an artist, and he looked at the world in the heartfelt and open way creative souls do. Painting was his medium and one of his works hangs in our upstairs hallway. He was one of the most curious people I knew and the most grateful. He loved to engage in conversations about consciousness (more than I often did!) and the fundamental forces in the universe. He saw beauty and wonder everywhere, be it in the cosmos or the forests and fields that surrounded his country home. And he was grateful for it all. I think curiosity and the love of learning were the biggest things we shared. The question I most often asked him was "What are you reading now?" His eyes would always sparkle as he launched into the telling.

The last words I said to him were "May you walk in beauty my friend."[7] I hope he heard me as my voice was cracked by emotion. I think he would appreciate the sentiment as he spent his whole life doing just that.

To me, friendship has a reflective and refractile quality. You can only know yourself in relation to others. You are reflected back to yourself by another human being. For most of us, the most illuminating discoveries are with and from friends. It's a co-creative process. I'm here because they are. It is, of course, not always smooth sailing. Relationships never are, but in the cornucopia of friendships we have in our lifetime, they all—in small, large, or unfathomable ways—irrevocably transform us into who we end up being.

---

7 "May you walk in beauty" is a Navajo phrase referring to the concept of *hózhó*, meaning the spiritual path of "the beauty way" or "walking in beauty." It celebrates life's sacredness, being in balance with and understanding nature's deep wisdom, and remembering the light within each person.

The light that imbues friendship passes through a prism that disperses the colors of who we are. From the featureless white light comes red, orange, yellow, green, blue, and violet. We discover we are not just one thing, but are many things, richly layered and changing over time's long road.

Loss of a friend shines the light in our eyes and reminds us of the many colors that linger, glowing softly in our friend and seeing our own reflected back. It calls us to remember who they were and who we are and be grateful that, for a time, together, we both walked in beauty.

ENDNOTE

A wonderful mystery to name is how our writing became our teacher, uncovering inner knowing that had been hidden from view. It happened often that what we wrote taught us in unexpected ways. We came up with writing prompts from a sense of "rightness." Yet, as we commented to each other many times, we did not know what we were going to write until we put pen to paper. Important connections were often waiting just under the surface of consciousness. In this chapter, for instance, we realized the vital links between friendships and belonging. And in telling our stories, we recognized our own journeys towards living authentic, undivided lives. We found we were making a more coherent meaning of our lives. Each of us. In parallel.

To be able to plumb the depths and heights of our life journeys is part of the gift of our friendship together. We have given each other the structure, space, trust, and unblinking affirmation to write our stories, to go deeper than we knew possible, and to share on the page what has shaped us. We have chosen each other as first witnesses of our stories. We didn't know we had it in us when we started. And now, two-thirds through our year of writing, we felt we had found our writing voices, uncovered ever-stronger threads, discovered new avenues that opened by turning to beauty, music, art, and movement as catalysts—handholds of head, heart, and soul! We were eager to see what unknown possibilities still lay ahead.

> ... the ultimate touchstone of friendship is not improvement, neither of the other nor of the self, the ultimate touchstone is witness, the privilege of having been seen by someone and the equal privilege of being granted the sight of the essence of another, to have walked with them and to have believed in them, and sometimes just to have accompanied them for however brief a span, on a journey impossible to accomplish alone.

David Whyte from "Friendship" in *Consolations*

CHAPTER NINE

Holding a Hand

**ON RECEIVING FATHER AT JFK AIRPORT AFTER HIS
LONG FLIGHT FROM KASHMIR**

As I fling my arms wide, he extends his hand.

Rafiq Kathwari

Ten words, just ten in Rafiq Kathwari's poem, but it opened so many possibilities. It made us laugh at first because of the social awkwardness, reminding us of times when we extended an arm for a handshake that wasn't returned. We also wondered about a strained father-son relationship perhaps made worse if one had been changed by a new and different culture. Before our online writing, the poem took us down the path of nonverbal greeting customs in different cultures. A handshake here, a kiss on the cheek (perhaps both cheeks) there, a hug, a bow—a veritable minefield for the uninitiated. And yet, what and how we communicate with our bodies (facial expression, eye contact, gestures, touch, tone of voice, etc.) transcends any words we may utter. The research is clear on this.

Over 80% of communication is nonverbal. Of all the nonverbal ways we relate to each other, touch is one of the most powerful. The skin is our largest sense organ, and we need to be touched as infants and children to foster healthy development. Nobody describes the centrality of touch better than Margaret Atwood, who said, "Touch comes before sight, before speech. It is the first language, and the last, and it always tells the truth."

Sometimes touch is awkward or unexpected. Our online stories were of that variety. Where you are, who you're with, and the passage of time open or close us in using our bodies to touch, to hold, or to hug our way into connection and communication. In the poem, we couldn't help wondering how the experience of a different culture may have affected how he greeted his father. Our online writing prompt arose from that curiosity.

PENNY ONLINE
A time you were changed by the culture you found yourself in.

When I had the chance to do some work in Kenya, I learned about several cultural norms it would be respectful to follow. One was in meeting and greeting someone. The practice was to shake another's hand with one hand and then place your other hand over both of your clasped hands, closing the circle of greeting so that a welcoming enclosure was created. I tried it and realized it felt complete. It made me mindful in a way that a taken-for-granted handshake did not.

It might have been a disused practice, since I noticed several times when I did this my Kenyan colleagues gave a small start and then placed their own second hand on both of mine. It almost felt like an afterthought, a remembered tradition brought back by a guest. I was never sure.

In the midst of many cultural differences, what unexpectedly created connections in Kenya was smiling. I had been in other cultures where smiling was suspect until you were known. Not so here. I am an easy smiler, and all of the Kenyan people I met had beautiful, wide smiles—white teeth gleaming against smooth dark skin. I wanted to smile ever more in response to that beauty, and it seemed reciprocal. I have always used smiling to convey interest and friendliness, and it did that here.

The two-handed handshake never became natural, yet I continued offering it as a mark of respect. I hope it was taken in that way and not as some pretentious "white person" trying on a different behavior.

DARCY ONLINE
A time you were changed by the culture you found yourself in.

I walked up to Tony and without a word hugged him. I don't generally hug people. I hadn't seen him in over 10 years, and this was a horrible time. Shelley and I had traveled to Colorado to attend the memorial event for his 13-year-old daughter, who had died by suicide a few weeks prior. Words can't hold that, but arms might.

The hug caught me by surprise as much as it did Tony—a non-demonstrative Brit if there ever was one. It felt right for me, and I think it felt right for Tony. A few years prior to this I wouldn't have done it. I would not have opened myself up emotionally to receive Tony in that way or to receive myself.

The community and the culture that allowed that growth to happen was created by the Courage & Renewal work I had experienced in the previous two years. The deep welcome and acceptance I had received broke down inner barriers that had been firmly built. It was an awakening of sorts. If they could accept me as who I was, well I must be worthy enough to accept myself.

I found a firm foundation and standing on that growth; I could open and be vulnerable in ways that I had never been. In this instance, it showed up as a big bear hug for a friend who needed it.

WHAT GOES AROUND COMES AROUND

On this day of writing together, as usual, we wrote online for 15 minutes. Depending on how long it took us to find a way into the prompt (what thread to pick up and follow), the writing could be but a brief snapshot of a thought that arose. It was sometimes a mere beginning and then it ended. Yet, in more than one writing session, that online snapshot ushered in a train of images and memories that took us to a related topic and led to richer and more expansive at-home writing.

That was the case here. Our at-home writing spoke to more personal and intimate experiences. We share some individual thoughts as we revisit our writing for that week.

ON REFLECTION . . .

PENNY

Even now, recalling this one Kenyan experience I can still feel the awkwardness of "trying on" an unfamiliar behavior in a culture that was brand new to me, and being received with some hesitancy in return. It is a snippet of memory, yet the slightly unsettling impact remains. Maybe there was more to say in the writing, but the time was up. I let it go.

It is perhaps no wonder that for our at-home writing I turned to a loving and reciprocal experience of holding hands. It is a good reminder that what may seem an unfinished story may simply be a warmup for what is to come. It is also possible that a first glimpse of an event told in a brief foray may yield richer reflections later.

I am only now rereading my Kenyan handshake story, over a year later. I am thinking about what is "acceptable" in the physical showing of respect, friendship, or affection. It has been an ongoing learning that what is natural and welcome for me may be quite different for others.

I have found it easiest to let go of assumptions (say, about hugging, handshakes, and smiling) when I'm visiting a new culture, as I know I have a lot to learn. When my work or travel for pleasure brought me to other countries, I tried to be a careful observer of what physical behaviors were practiced and accepted and act accordingly. My hosts have been kind in teaching me. Sometimes they have teased me, a friendly sign that we were on the right path. (Thank goodness I can laugh at myself.) I have found that showing up with a good heart goes a long way in forging mutual respect and in forgiving missteps that inevitably occur.

The more unexpected learning has been here at home. I used to think that any friend would welcome a hug. With some surprise, I observed early on that Jim was not comfortable being hugged, except by me or a few very close friends. He didn't grow up with that kind of physical affection and was more naturally reserved. His affections ran deep; he just showed them differently. Loving him taught me to respect and admire that difference in him and then to be more aware of it in others.

I remember an incident that touched me deeply. I was leading a week-long course for physician educators. As part of that experience, our group of twelve participants met daily for two hours to reflect on core experiences in their work and lives. Trust and affectionate regard had developed, and people felt able to share very personal stories. One participant (I'll call him Carl) told us that he grew up in a military family and could not remember ever being hugged or even touched as a child. He had never become comfortable with the easy hugging of others, including at this course. We held his story in respectful silence.

In the last session of our group, Carl told us how much the week had meant to him. He said he had shared some experiences for the first time and felt warmly received and accepted. In a very low voice, he added, "If anyone wants to give me a small hug, I guess that would be okay."

My heart broke a little, in a good way. Some things you never forget.

DARCY

When I reread my story of hugging Tony, it seemed like a brief sidelong glance. A glimmer of something larger. That fleeting contact was a powerful one in my memory. Thinking back, I did not know I had changed until my body told me. Being hugged or seeing others hugging was a rare occurrence growing up. My body remembered how it felt, however. A warm, smothering, love-filled hug by an aunt as I stood shivering after a lake swim lingers still. The shift and my willingness to step forward with arms flung wide to see others and see myself was lodged, forgotten and undetected in my bones.

Touch and loss showed up in my online writing and also in my at-home story about my mother. This was unintentional, but the emotional ripples of the online piece no doubt took me to another even more impactful recollection. Contributing to this feeling was that my story of Tony was just one piece of a wider somber picture.

I didn't realize that encounter would be the last time I saw or spoke to Tony. He felt surprisingly small and diminished when I hugged him. Tony was always a bit shorter than me, but he seemed withered by his grief, as if his life force was being inexorably drained. He had and would experience other losses. A divorce a few years prior, and then being let go from a treasured high-status job a few months after his only child's death, were too much. Tony died six months after I saw him, in circumstances that made me think he took his own life after losing so much that gave his own purpose and fulfillment. A tragic closure to a sad, final life chapter—a life that intersected mine for many years early in my professional career as we worked closely together as friends and colleagues.

Out of that space filled with Tony's grief and loss, and my unexpected hug, emerged another experience I felt compelled to write about, one that I had to make real in the way only writing it down can. My at-home writing would be about the last time I held my mother's hand.

WHEN TOUCH COMES NATURALLY

When we turned to creating our at-home writing prompt, it was the poem's last word, "hand," that called to us. It is such a powerful symbol. Hands operationalize our intentions by touching the world we live in. They give and receive help, reassurance, affection, anger, violence, food, friendship, love, and much more. So, for our at-home assignment, we asked ourselves the simple and obvious question: what does it mean to touch another and hold someone's hand?

PENNY AT-HOME
A story of holding someone's hand.

These days my stories of holding someone's hands are metaphorical. I have so many sick friends or friends in distress for various reasons. I find myself holding them in my heart, accompanying them with my listening, my sadness, my compassion. It is the beautiful, painful reality of love that friends will suffer, and some will die (of course all will die, but not necessarily on my watch). And being a friend means bearing that suffering as a witness, as a companion, and by holding their hands in real and imagined ways.

But today I will write in more depth about a story of Jim and me holding hands. After all, it is his birthday. He would have been 87 today.

We held hands all the time. On every walk. I particularly loved the feeling of being together in that simple, loving way. One summer we vacationed again in Wellfleet on Cape Cod, a favorite place. That year we splurged and stayed in an ocean-front cottage. The beach was right there outside our door a few hundred yards away, and we took long oceanside walks every morning. I remember one particular morning. We were walking, holding hands, laughing, looking out at the ocean, same as always. A young man was walking towards us, yet far higher up on the beach. He veered in our direction and walked diagonally across the sand to reach us. When he approached, he said he had watched us many times walking on the beach and holding hands. He wanted to tell us how much that touched him.

I was moved. Holding hands was so natural, it was automatic. I'm not sure I knew how special it was until it was mirrored back to us. It spoke of love and intimacy in a way I hadn't named before. It made me happy to be witnessed. Jim, who was much shyer, might have been embarrassed to be "seen" in this way. I don't remember him saying. It didn't stop us, thank goodness. We always held hands, and we laughed a lot.

I liked dropping hands to walk apart for a while—perhaps because a mountain path was too narrow, or because being alone is as precious as coming back together. Each supports the other in the dance of life.

Who reached for the beloved's hands? I have a feeling I was more the reacher, as I am naturally more expressive of emotion than Jim was. Yet it was our habit and a great comfort to be met in this way.

Happy birthday, Jim. I honor our years and am grateful for the physical memory of our hands entwined on all those paths.

DARCY AT-HOME
A story of holding someone's hand.

When I put my hand on hers, it was warm, surprisingly so since the life that had lived in my mother for 93 years was barely a glimmer. It was like the last flare of a candle flame before it sputters out. I let my hand rest on hers for a few minutes. It was a hand that I had touched or held since infancy. It still had the elegance I remember despite the withered flesh and recent bruising from blood sampling. I'm not sure she was aware of my hand on hers. She did not move or turn her head. Her closed eyes fluttered briefly. That was enough. She was in her own world now. On that final journey that would end a few days later.

I like to think she was sifting through old memories. Turning the pages of a well-curated photo album. Smiling at this and that and saying hello and goodbye to all the people she had known and sights she'd seen. Packaging things up neat and tidy before she left. Something she always did in her day-to-day life.

I couldn't keep my hand on hers for long. The intensity of that connection and knowing this was the final time I would touch my mother, coupled with her seemingly urgent need to keep moving and not be distracted, made me pull my hand away. It was like standing close to a raging fire (of emotions, of final goodbyes, of ruthless inevitabilities). You could only take it for a short time.

I continued to sit by her bedside for another hour or so. My mind, like hers, gently turning over pages of my own photo album of memories. Accepting all of who she was at her worst and at her best. All is forgiven now. The slate has been wiped clean. We can just sit here. I smile and hold her in a misted gaze. No words are necessary or needed. We both know that everything will be okay.

TURNING A CORNER

Now, 11 months after our year of writing together, we reflect on our deep dive into poignant memories of touch. We are struck by the immediacy of "presence" evoked in both of our stories. For each of us, this was a recounting of exquisite presence as a part of loss. What would arise if we invited an experience of joyful presence? We decided to see.

PENNY
A story of joyful presence.

I look out my living room window at the breaking dawn. The sky is pearl gray. Subtle rose pink is playing on the glass sky-scraper with its triangular roof just across the way—the iconic building I have come to know at every time of day and in all seasons. Trains are on the move and the highways below are already choc-a-bloc with traffic. To the southwest, I can see two of the five bridges that span the Schuylkill River. Tiny lights frame their arches and in the still-dark morning, the yellow rays are reflected in the calm ribbon of the river. It is a Currier and Ives painting set in a city, an urban landscape that is unexpectedly compelling and beautiful.

The first time I saw this view that was to become home was just over two years ago. The moment and the scene are seared in my memory. After four years of grieving Jim's loss and the strange, life-stopping time of the COVID pandemic, I was turning to new openings, new choices, new life. To my wonder, I had met a kindred partner, David, and we decided in a matter of months to create a life together. Our plan was to move from our respective homes of many decades to a one-story apartment in Center City, Philadelphia.

The search for a new home felt exciting, daunting, courageous, and unknown—a claim to possibility, aliveness, and love in this fourth season of our lives. At moments in the quest, I became acutely aware of how much beauty of place mattered to me. I longed, too, for a view—a visual way to imagine the future I was stepping into, to feel a sense of homecoming.

We walked through the front door of this apartment with its light-filled rooms and spacious windows. I was riveted by the river, the city, the view. My heart knew it had landed. What I saw was a metaphor for what my life could be, would be—a ribbon of calm threading through the colorful chaos of urban life, a tapestry of movement and pattern. I knew I would be learning the particularities of this landscape for a long time. I sensed that it would hold me.

In that instant, I stepped into a new era, a new city, a new partnership, a new life—joyfully present to what would unfold.

DARCY
A Story of Joyful Presence

A flash of red caught the corner of my eye as I bent over to find something in the back of the SUV. I turned and was surprised to see a Tibetan Buddhist monk in their characteristic, burgundy-colored robes, casually strolling by. Surprised because Shelley and I were in Boulder, Utah, a small town (pop. 243) on the edge of the 1.9 million-square-acre Grand Staircase-Escalante National Monument. In the middle of not much else and nestled in Mormon ranch country.

We were staying at the Boulder Mountain Lodge, one of the nicer accommodations in the area, but principally because of a special restaurant, Hell's Backbone Grill. As it turns out, the restaurant owners were Buddhist, and every year, they invited monks to spend time at the Lodge. This area and other canyonlands across southern Utah hold a treasured place in both my and Shelley's hearts. The arid, lonely quiet of the expansive, colorful mesas and canyons centers and grounds us. We seem to come home to ourselves. So, it makes sense that spiritual visitors were brought to, and found connection, to this spirit-filled land.

Boulder is also the start of the Burr Trail, a 67-mile road through ochre-painted canyons and dry flatlands that ends precipitously on the top of the Waterpocket Fold, a monumental rock reef running 100 miles in a north-south direction and part of Capitol Reef National Park. From the top, you descend through a series of steep graveled switchbacks before you reach the valley floor. It can be a white-knuckle ride even if you are in a four-wheel-drive vehicle.

Just before you descend the switchbacks, though, is a nondescript turnoff that looks like more of an afterthought than a road. There is a small blue picnic-table sign on a tilting stake at the entrance. It was this sign that caused us to veer off the road. After all, we had a picnic cooler full of lunch items and it was that time of day. In short course, the road ended abruptly, with nothing in sight except for a small narrow trail leading up to a couple of windblown, stunted trees.

At the end of the trail, we could see a weathered picnic table hidden by the trees and perched on a cliff above the descending switchbacks. The view looked north along the Waterpocket Fold, showing the jagged reef-like wall of the Fold to our left and the mottled, brick-brown arid Strike Valley to our right. It continued uninterrupted for as far as our eyes could see. Light gusts and swirls of wind tugged at us as we stood speechless in the bright midday sun. We both quietly sat at the picnic table, bags full of lunch items dangling limply at our sides.

We were sitting, but I think we were really kneeling in recognition of the beauty and sacredness of that still and quiet land. It filled us. In that moment there was nothing but awe and wonder. We were subsumed into the wildness of the terrain, melting into it somehow knowing that, in our own way, it lived in us and always had. Discovering that we were connected, made from the same elemental alchemy that created the magnificence we beheld, we felt big and small at the same time. This was our soul's truth. We could hear it, a clear and resonant hymn, in this, one of nature's most transcendent cathedrals.

SIMPLE QUESTIONS, IMPORTANT STORIES

Rachel Naomi Remen wrote that "facts bring us to knowledge, but stories lead to wisdom." In this chapter we gave ourselves simple writing prompts, "Tell a story about . . . " The responses, however, were more than straightforward or simple. They captured moments and how we remembered them. In the telling, or writing, we enlarged the image we had of our worlds and ourselves. Stories are the crucible for meaning-making. We all use stories to weave ourselves into the tapestry of our experiences in ways that make sense to us and to who we were or are becoming.

Hands, hugging, loss, and joy. They all belong together and showed up in our stories, illustrating the wisdom that lives in our bodies (the theme of chapter 5, "Words and Beyond Words"). It also reveals how we use our bodies to feel our way forward and into connection and communion. Stories are collections of words that aspire to capture what lives in and flows between bodies. Sometimes, all we need is to hold a hand or be hugged. No words necessary.

> And here's the fork in the road
> to an entire life: Do we focus
> on the difficulty of the climb or
> the magnificence of the view?

For me, I honored the climb
and praised the view, and was
somehow returned to wanting
only warmth and only to be
held.

Mark Nepo from "Over the Ridge"

CHAPTER TEN

Presence of Absence

that he had every right to be at peace
on whatever ground he walked.

Esteban Rodriguez from "22: La Bota"

Naturalist and conservationist John Muir aptly observed that "When we try to pick out anything by itself, we find it hitched to everything else in the universe." He had a lifelong love affair with the Sierra Nevada mountains in southern California and was largely responsible for the creation of Yosemite National Park and Sequoia National Park. Connection is the energetic glue that binds us and everything else (plant, animal, rock) together in a time-bound waltz to diverse and different rhythms.

Connection to place, to others, to ourselves, has been a thread running through the last two chapters. It is a universal human need. We require anchor points to tether and hold us steady in the swirling currents of our lives. They can be partners, friends, family, animals, the tree in our backyard, and for many of us, the very ground we walk on.

In this chapter, we got inspiration for our online writing by reading the poem "22: La Bota" by Esteban Rodríguez.

This visceral description of a troubled father and his work boots ends with "he had every right to be at peace on whatever ground he walked." The words "peace" and the "ground he walked" were irresistible, especially as they evoked connection and our quest to find it. The online writing prompt we came up with spoke to that. Occasionally, a poem will lead to an obvious prompt, at times almost literally, as was the case here. A gift we were happy to receive.

PENNY ONLINE
When do you feel at home on the ground you walk?

I love when I get to know a place well enough to call it home, to feel at ease and at peace in walking its familiar turns and straightaways. I'm thinking of a network of paths, paved and wooded, as well as wilder places I've come to know. It starts for me with the deciduous woodlands of the Northeast United States. I grew up here, and even though I've lived in other parts of the country, this land will forever be "home."

Having a place where much is anticipated conjures up safety and delight in its familiarity, like the dip in the path leading down to the water of Stony Run creek, or the way that cherry tree from down the block looks in its first bloom of spring, or the glowing gold leaves of the sugar maple on Wyndhurst Avenue in autumn. Then, when the superstructure is in place, I am open to see the nuances of the unexpected. Bringing fresh eyes to my known world is a special delight. New sightings are a surprise.

Of course, there are also the yearly pleasures of transient sightings—like the warblers coming through in spring. I remember one black-throated blue warbler in particular that took my breath away, or the way the myriad brilliantly colored leaves made a memorable picture, fallen on the street and glistening wet from rain—a tapestry of fall beauty.

To know a place yet turn to wonder is always a gift of surprises.

My feet know the feel of certain places—a literal case of feeling at home on the ground I walk: the sand on the beach of the dunes in Sandwich, Cape Cod, the riverwalk in my new city of Philadelphia where I have learned the feel of asphalt, cobbles, and dirt as I make my way along the Schuylkill River path.

ON REFLECTION . . .

PENNY
Feeling at Home on New Ground

Sometimes I feel unexpectedly at home in a new place, connected in a larger way to all of life. Such was my experience on a visit one summer to Cornwall, England. Here is what I wrote then, as part of our year of writing, yet from a faraway place.

We already have favorite places in Fowey, England. How amazing to be a stranger one day and feel at home a few days later. We took the locally acclaimed circular Hall Walk, starting with the short ferry ride across the Fowey River and proceeding along the estuary; up and down hills, many very steep, with gorgeous glimpses of green water and anchored sailboats below, all in their bright canvas covers—and beyond them, the pastel houses pasted against the hillsides. We heard and saw the now-familiar chiffchaffs, singing their repetitive song as a backup to the ever-present wrens, like a two-bird improv band.

What do I see when I view this land here in Fowey? I see history.

I feel my own history more acutely here, and how my story weaves together with the countless stories of all who have gone before and are going along now and will come in the future. There is a comfort here in being part of the passage of years; a rightness that we each get our allotment of time, live it fully if we are lucky and mindful, and then give way for the next travelers.

There are fine needles of mist on my face and hands as I walk on this foggy, cloudy day along the coast of St. Mawes, wood pigeons my constant companion and the European goldfinch, dunnock, and ever-present gulls as background music. Every name has charm: chaffinch, chiffchaff, stonechat, jackdaw! A child's fairy tale waiting to be told. On the water, a small sailboat is making its way in the slight breeze. Ahead, a two-person motorboat chugs along, and a larger sailboat motors past it into port. It is a gentle, quiet morning.

"History is now and England." Maybe I'm beginning to understand what T.S. Eliot was saying. As I look at this land, I imagine hundreds of years of stories and of the people who have left their mark in land and architecture, in signs and gardens and remnants of events and lives lived, wars fought, lands tilled, births and deaths of family upon family. But also, I see my own history.

Memories of other travels to this country come to me. I am looking out at the sea and hedgerow fields in their neat squares, and I am suddenly with Jim. He is just around the corner, always ahead of me, exploring, seeing man-made artifacts I would have missed. Or I am with Lynn on our trip to Ireland or Wales, the curve of a hill with glorious pink flowers and wild grasses and beyond it the sea—bringing back those other times.

I am younger. I am my age. I am older. My life is peeling away behind me and through me and beyond. This place will go on after me. It has long preceded me. I am in it for my brief moments—lucky, alive, a visitor and yet, unexpectedly, at home.

DARCY ONLINE
When do you feel at home on the ground you walk?

I'm home when I can show up as myself. When the welcome or invitation is genuine and includes all of you. Not just the good bits, the sense of humor, the kindness, or the expertise. All of it, including the stuff that you're not proud of. The barriers, the detachment, impatience, and insecurities. It happens when I'm with my wife, Shelley, close friends, and family, particularly my sister.

Siblings have shared ground that has been walked on in many seasons, over many years. They have seen you and you have seen them at the best and worst times. Fought with them, cried with them, and laughed with them. No preconditions. Nothing qualified or held back. You moved through your lives together, freely choosing your own paths but always aware of the paths they were taking. Making sure that you showed up for the important things. Births, deaths, graduations, funerals, and sometimes rescues. At a time when our parents' marriage was coming undone, and bitterness and contempt were served for breakfast, lunch, and dinner, my recently married sister (six years my senior) would gather me up and take me away on camping trips to the Rocky Mountains of Alberta and British Columbia. Anything to remove me from the toxicity and forlornness of what home had become. We walked on new ground together for the coming years— and still do.

I know I'm where I belong when I'm with my sister. When we visit, I can sit on the couch and her on a chair. We may talk, or we may not. We can go for a walk and share the challenges or rewards of our lives, or not. We're okay just being together. It doesn't need words; we've shared too much to pretend.

ON REFLECTION . . .

_____

DARCY
The Ground You Are Born Into

There is the home within yourself, the spiritual sanctuary that is the nourishing aquifer of your power and purpose, and there is the physical home, a landscape that you recognize as a place of beginnings, a place you can touch, see, and smell. The physical home can expand or contract depending on your experiences and life stage. At no time is the clarity of that home so sharp and crystalline as when you come to know it as a child.

I grew up in a suburban style bungalow in the quiet end of Brown Street just before it curves to join Albert Street, in the northwest corner of a small prairie city called Moose Jaw, situated in southern Saskatchewan, Canada. I spent all my childhood and teenage years living in that house and neighborhood.

My father built the house in what was, in 1959, a new development. We moved in during the winter of 1960 when I was still a baby and my sister was six years old. Just looking at the house, you could place the era of its construction. It had baby-blue-colored wood siding on the lower half of the exterior, while the upper half was covered with "bottle dash" (also known as "beer bottle," "broken bottle," or "crushed bottle") stucco, a unique building technique popular on homes built in western Canada in the 1950s and 60s. It consisted of an applied layer of mortar to which broken brown and green colored glass chips were embedded, mostly from recycled beer and pop bottles.

If you were lucky, you could make out the brand of pop or beer. I found fragments of 7- Up pop and Bohemian beer bottles. Only as a kid do you have the time and patience to look that closely. The stucco was like armor and lasted forever with little maintenance. It was also a hazard to rambunctious children. If you were pushed or fell against it, deep scrapes and blood ensued.

Streets, avenues, and crescents (Caribou, Carleton, Albert, Hopkins, Grayson, 11th, 12th, 13th, and Simpson) that surrounded my house were walked and cycled countless times. You knew where all the cracks in the sidewalks were or if there was too much sand on the road for you to take a fast right turn on your bicycle from Simpson Avenue onto Brown Street (city buses turned left here and would leave small berms of sand and gravel, especially in early spring after a winter of sand application to battle icy roads). You knew which fences were safe to climb over to take a shortcut, and where the dogs were who would bark and chase you was well mapped and understood by my friends.

I drove by my old house a year ago, ten years after my mother moved out. The siding is now a darker blue, but the bottle dash stucco still looks as good as the day it was put on. The trees are bigger and some of the same sidewalk cracks and rough roads are still there. It's always a strange experience cruising through these well-trod spaces. Memories slide by as I do. The names of families that lived near you, the other kids you played with, and the trouble you got into (the house where your friend broke the living room picture window with a puck while playing hockey on their driveway, the piece of road where you nearly got run over by a car when the wagon you were being towed in by your friend on his bike veered off the sidewalk and into traffic, the place where you found a $20 bill in the snowbank).

It's a luxury of childhood to see that clearly, to have memories and an orientation to your early living landscape forever etched in your being. To absorb that wide, large world in all its colors and textures. As an adult looking back, I'm wistful for that clarity, that close noticing and sense of largeness, the never forgetting. I may not belong to that neighborhood anymore, but that ground will always be inside me.

I know where I came from. When somebody asks where I grew up, I tell them "Moose Jaw," and they say, "Really! That's an interesting name," and I say, "Yes, it is, let me tell you about it (in great detail)."

THE FRUITFULNESS OF EXPLORING OPPOSITES

In the last chapter (and that weekly writing session), we explored "presence." We now turned our attention to its necessary counterpart, "absence," for our at-home writing, having discovered the power of exploring opposites.

Nothing, emptiness, pause, space, stillness, silence. The Japanese concept of *Ma* speaks to emptiness full of possibility and the need to have space to breathe, feel, and connect to life. It has been described as the pure and essential void in all things. In art, Ma shows up as negative space that surrounds and defines an object. It is the pause between words in a conversation or the notes in music, or it may define the essence of things (the space in a pot not the container, the inside of a house not the walls and roof). It is the vital space that gives things their meaning, their usefulness.

In our conversations during the writing of this book (and designing retreats), we have often talked about the importance of unfilled space, pauses, or absences, and how important they are to fully understand and appreciate how we inhabit and are present to our own lives. It's a compelling and sometimes heartbreaking paradox. We are present, but the absent partner, parent, friend, or stranger seems to surround and define our time and space. They are intermingled. Absence contains presence. How we come to see and hold the open landscapes of our experiences is a life's journey. One that is filled with inevitable losses but much beauty too.

We were curious to discover what our forays into "the presence of absence" would uncover.

PENNY AT-HOME
When has the presence of absence moved you?

It's the mounting number of anticipated and all-too-horrifically imagined deaths that have me in their grip these days. I'm talking about dear friends who are facing the end, as well as strangers who seem like friends. I can't get them out of my mind—the Israeli and Palestinian girls and boys, men and women—snuffed out, mid-joy, mid-life, mid-dailiness and dancing and talking and eating and taking long walks. Their aborted laughter haunts me.

There is a counterpoint to that pain. The beauty of the presence of those dear ones no longer here fills me with love and gladness. My wonderful friend Rig (25 years my senior when she lived, and now gone for 25 years) still shows up when I open a cookbook she gave me or upon remembering her making me eggs six different ways when I stayed with her for a week. She was with me every day for years. I'd think of her at random times—impossible to believe she wasn't here any longer except in vivid memory.

That will be true of Jim forever. He moves me almost daily. Yesterday I said something he always said and smiled—no need to explain. It was just a "Jim-ism" that made an ordinary event funny. Okay, I'll say it, but it won't make anyone else smile. When we bought bread, he called it "breadskies." See, I told you. But it doesn't matter. He makes me smile a lot, and he's been gone for over five years.

His walk is ingrained in my mind; I can call it up in a heartbeat. He put one hand on his hip and strode down any street, unmistakable even from afar—and I'm nearsighted! There is also his smile. Is, was. Time has no meaning when a beloved absent one is so present. Past becomes now and moves seamlessly into the future. The pain of acute grief has morphed into sweetness and a surprising sense of time-less reality.

Not so with my friend J., who has been given two years to live; or my friend K., who will fade away at some unknown rate from Alzheimer's, or the husband of my friend who is on death's door and so very present now as they grab every second and know it is precious. These absences loom larger than presence and are "moving" in an unbearable horrible sense. Moved to tears. Moved to screams. Moved to inaction and waiting.

I must mention, also, the night hawks. I lived in my beau-tiful home in Baltimore for 35 years, and for at least 25 of those I relished looking up into the sky at dusk when I heard the plaintive calls of the night hawks. There they would be, swooping high in the sky, catching insects on the wing as the light faded. They were a constant and delightful presence. Then they disappeared. Who knows why? Insecticides? Cli-mate change? Yet they were ingrained in my idea of evening and in my memory, so that even years later I found myself looking up, willing the presence of those small hawk-shaped wings and that descending call. I could say the same for fireflies that used to be thick in late Baltimore summers— thousands of flashing points of light in the warm August nights, now only a few ghostly flickers evoking memories.

They too live in my mind's eye. It is not enough. I feel their presence. I live their absence.

DARCY AT-HOME
When has the presence of absence moved you?

Sand peppered my face and eyes as wind gusts scoured the dune crest. I struggled up the slope, feet half buried, sliding and being covered by yet more sand. An alien in an alien landscape. Bereft of the usual adornments like towering trees, majestic mountains, cooling lakes, and verdant green carpets. Just sand, defiant withered shrubs, and me. This is the Great Sand Hills in the prairies of southwestern Saskatchewan. The region of my birth. Nineteen hundred square kilometers of harsh land within another. This is a land of absences, and like most things, it's relative. No in-your-face beauty here, but beauty nonetheless for those curious and open enough to see it, hear it, feel it, and know it in your nose. Sharp aromas lifted on impatient breezes mirror the hard places that life clings to.

There is something sacred about desolate and delicate lands. They get by despite the absences and create their own beauty by doing so. They invented minimalism before it was a word, before there were words. Each blade of grass, resolute sagebrush, or battered tree stands defiantly on their own sustaining ground separate from, but intertwined with, the lives of foxes, mule deer, Ord's kangaroo rats, and pronghorn antelope. All living in this precarious borderland, not a prairie, not a desert, something that is its own. A landscape where life is stretched thin and laid tentatively on the dunes and in-between places.

I feel many restless spirits coursing between the dunes, caressing the grass, and drawing dreams in the sand. Questions carried on the wind whisper. Who am I in this place? Where do I end, and this land begin? Am I worthy to be here? How do I pay my respects and bear witness to its story?

I must be on my way soon. As I climb down the dune, my shoes fill with stardust. The scent of sage floats by, reminding me that I'm part of this landscape and I belong in it just as it belongs in me. My heart settles in this wondrous place of struggle and absence. I smile. It's too soon to leave. I'll just sit here a while longer and talk with my friends, the restless spirits. We'll laugh and all tell each other how beautiful we are!

ENDNOTE

Our writing uncovered the shifting tides of presence flowing into absence, returning to presence. There is a wholeness to this exquisite paradox. Our lives—all life—contains both presence and absence, what is and what was, current reality and memory, what is there and what is missing. We have discovered that it is not only necessary but essential to explore both aspects. In holding both realities up to the light, we honor the completeness of our lived experiences.

As had happened before, when we read our stories to each other we were deeply moved by what each other wrote. Somewhat unexpectedly, reading aloud and being so warmly received also opened us more profoundly to our own emotions—to feelings that we may have held in check or that lived just out of our awareness. Receiving the powerful gifts of being seen, held, and affirmed by the other, we let ourselves more completely into our own knowing. Our connection is, indeed, the magic hidden in plain sight that underpins our process. We acknowledge to each other with gratitude the manifold gifts of partnering on this writing journey.

To be human is to live with paradox
and hold it in our hands.

Parker J. Palmer

CHAPTER ELEVEN

What Shapes Us

I think of your hands all those years ago

Tracy K. Smith from "Song"

The stories in this chapter swept us into memories of things that made us, shaped us, scoured us, and polished us—parents, mentors, teachers, and self-discovery. It all started with the first line of Tracy K. Smith's poem "Song" that says, "I think of your hands all those years ago." We encountered "hands" for a second time in our writing, having explored this topic initially in chapter 9. The integral potency of this symbol sparked a second and equally impactful foray into our past and our parents, whose hands were the first ones we experienced beyond our own.

Without question, parents have an outsized role in our early development and heavily influence how we are launched into the adult world. Our memories of them exert a strong gravitational pull when we attempt to make coherent and meaningful connections to our past and present. Parents are a big part of our personal story, and it can get complicated to understand their influence, especially as we mature and move into later life stages. In his usual pithy style, Oscar Wilde said, "Children begin by loving their parents; after a time, they judge them; rarely, if ever, do they forgive them."

In homage to the poem's first line, we kept our online writing prompt simple and straightforward: "A memory of hands." It led to some rich discernment that, with the writing, reshaped in its own small way the image, understanding, gratitude, and compassion we felt—and maybe, some forgiveness we had—for our parents.

PENNY ONLINE
A memory of hands

My parents' hands informed my childhood. I can picture my mother and my father in my mind's eye, doing what they did every day—an enduring visual and auditory memory. The exquisite skill of their hands defined their lives.

Both of my parents were artists: music and art filled our home. Mama was a concert pianist and taught piano in our living room for many years. Even after her intense stage fright caused her to step away from performing, she still played her magnificent Steinway concert grand for hours a day. I have an indelible memory of her patience (playing the same passages over and over till they flowed) mixed with the beauty of the classical music she played—Chopin, Schubert, Beethoven, Mozart, Bach—all the great ones.

Papa was an Impressionist painter. He created compelling portraits of all of us in the family (my mother, himself, me, and my sister) and would include in his paintings renderings of great sculptures by Rodin or Michelangelo, or ancient Chinese scrolls. He loved architectural features: angles, windows, hallways. His paintings included intricate perspectives of distance and detail. I would often watch him as he painted, stepping forward to put a new mark on the canvas and stepping back far enough to see what he'd painted (being farsighted).

And too, my parents listened. They listened to us kids and they listened to each other. Every evening, we had dinner together, and they wanted to hear about what the day had been like for us.

We each got a turn. It was more than a download of events; they delighted in the details and the funny or hard things we saw or did. What we thought and felt mattered to them.

It was fun because my father often made limericks out of some name or incident Tina or I recounted. For instance, I would tell them about a girl named (I'm making this name up) April Rosencranz. My father would listen to my story and then make up a ditty that included the name and the high point. "There once was a girl named Rosencranz. She made a long face as she dropped her pants," or some such nonsense! (After he recited his limerick, Papa would laugh at his own humor till tears ran down his cheeks, and my mom would always respond in an amused, fake-exasperated voice, "Oh, Bill." His laughing at his own wordplay was the best part.)

I wanted to remember the nuances of my day to have them mirrored back in such a jolly way. After we children went to bed, they would sit up talking and listening to each other for a long time. I could hear their low murmurs and the interest in their tones of voice. I often made myself stay awake and went into the living room, saying I couldn't sleep, so I could get in on these grown-up conversations.

My mother died when I was 21. I can still see her hands playing and the set of her mouth as she leaned over the keys, willing her heart into the notes. My father died when I was 27. I can still see him lifting his brush to dip it into his palette of colors and place a new stroke on the painting, focused and graceful.

They loved ideas. They made art. Their visible lives and ways of being became a part of me, informed me, formed me, are with me still.

DARCY ONLINE
A memory of hands

I remember noticing my father's hands when I was a child. They were not large but compact, callused, and strong. My father's history was etched on them. How many board feet of lumber had those hands passed over, cut, shaped, and sanded? He worked with wood his whole life as a carpenter and as a teacher of carpentry. His hands also carried his childhood. Growing up always hungry on a hardscrabble homestead in southern Saskatchewan during the Dirty '30s (a time of drought and dust storms on the prairies and the Great Depression across the US and Canada).

He joined the Armed Forces at the beginning of World War II before he finished high school (only finishing many years after the war with the help and tutoring of my mother). His years working as a fitter in the Air Force were in his hands too. He told me of a time when they were installing steel plating behind the pilot's seat to protect them against strafing gunfire from fighter planes. The plate was very heavy, and my father was pushing hard to keep it in place while another fitter drilled in anchoring screws. One screw went through my father's hand, unnoticed until he tried to remove it. That time of war and special comradery also lived in my dad's hands. Or the time a block of ice crushed his right hand when he worked as a teenager loading boxcars in the Moose Jaw railyard. My father loved to tell stories. The same ones over and over and over again. All of them lived in his hands.

When my dad would hold my young hand, I could feel the capable, thick fingers and rough, cracked surfaces. Almost like they could have used some of the sandpaper he treated his woodworking projects to. His hands reflected who he was as a person and father. They shared the same characteristics. Rough, direct, but also generous. His right hand used to shake as he wrote. A remnant of the ice block trauma. His jerky, wavy-lined letters and words contrasted with the apparent skill and strength his hands had. He one-finger-typed his way through a teaching degree that just about killed him, or so it seemed, while surrounded by academically accomplished doctors and lawyers on my mother's side of the family. It was a vulnerability and insecurity that he never showed the world, but it and others showed up at home.

Those hands shaped my father's world and also shaped me. His hands helped him understand and make sense of his life and who he was, as do mine. I get deep, visceral satisfaction when touching and working with something, be it an animal, wood, or machinery. I think of him often when engaged in a carpentry project, and especially when I use one of his treasured tools that I inherited. His admonishments still run through my mind: "Darcy, if you don't have time to do it right the first time, do you have time to do it all over again?"

Growing up, I had a rocky relationship with him. Not uncommon for fathers and sons where expectations crash against aspirations. That softened with time, but we remained very different and yet similar. My dad's hands were a window to who he was and were every bit as complicated as he was. As we all are.

FINDING AN UNEXPECTED WRITING PROMPT

While the poem "Song" led easily to our shared online writing, it did not stimulate a question for our at-home writing. This was one of those weeks when we searched outside of our usual sources of poems and personal check-ins for a topic. This day, we looked to the weekly *Poetry Unbound* newsletter of Padraig O'Tuama for inspiration. That day, he had posed a question that hit a resonant chord: "What surprise has saved you? Made you?" We decided to use it as our writing prompt.

We were each taken by the unexpected pull of the question, both feeling a heightened sense of anticipation for what lay ahead.

––––––––––––––––

PENNY AT-HOME
What surprise has saved you? Made you?

I "met" Parker Palmer through the accident of a phone call. I didn't know I was looking for a way of thinking, teaching, and being that would change my life, that would over time become my life. I thought I was trying to find funding for an organization I led, and a mutual friend suggested I speak with Parker (whom I'd not heard of), as he was a senior advisor to a foundation that gave money to advance the human and spiritual dimensions of various professions. The friend said that I sounded a little like Parker when I talked about my work. So, I called Parker on the phone. Parker! I don't think email was a "thing" then, and I believe I just called.

I may have reached him the first time and then set up a time to talk. That is most likely how we met, although it was 30 years ago, and I can't say for sure. What I remember was the shift. What started out as a polite, engaged call about each of our work soon became a soulful exploration and sharing about how we experienced the world, of how that seeing informed our work.

The first surprise came when Parker said he thought the adult journey was about living an "undivided life." I didn't know what he meant by that phrase, but something that had been hidden inside me stirred, awakened, and I asked if he would say more. He said it was when how you felt on the inside was how you showed up on the outside. I felt a jolt of recognition. My world trembled.

I was at the time living a horribly divided life. I helped to lead an organization for physician continuing education. I loved the organization and its work, yet to stay and lead I felt I had to pretend to be someone else.

There was only one way to do things. The lack of freedom to innovate or shift in any direction was killing me on the inside, while to the outside world I showed only support, admiration, and acquiescence. I was a fully supportive, cheerful advocate, never making ripples. No one knew how I felt. There were enough wonderful things about what we were doing that I told myself time and again that it was worth it not to show up whole but simply carry out the work. It was not. When Parker used that expression, I knew I had to learn more about his work.

The second surprise was that Parker said yes when I invited him to experience one of our teaching courses as a participant. (As luck would have it, our summer course was to occur in his hometown of Madison, Wisconsin, and his schedule, remarkably, was clear for three of the four-and-a-half days.) During that week, Parker and four physician teachers made up the small group that I led for part of every day. That group practiced and reflected on various aspects of the medical encounter with patients—as clinicians and teachers and as patients, themselves. A memorable moment for me was when Parker shared openly and vulnerably about an earlier personal experience in that very hospital. It was an opening for me into the possibility of living in an undivided way. He felt something. He shared it. He didn't pretend all was well. And he was held in higher regard by the group because of it.

The third surprise was when Parker invited me to come to a two-day gathering to learn more about his work. It was held at the Fetzer Institute, which would be a major source of funding for this work.

I didn't know that Parker was looking to choose six people to teach and mentor from the 25 people he'd invited to this gathering. I didn't know I was being considered.

I remember I arrived 30 minutes late and entered the opening meeting a little breathless. The group was arranged in a large circle and individuals had just begun to introduce themselves. I knew I would be cutting the time close but couldn't get an earlier plane due to my teaching responsibilities. I'm not sure why I felt safe enough to speak so openly in my first sharing. Perhaps it was the circle, or the fact that we could speak when we felt ready, not in some predetermined order. Perhaps it was Parker's warm welcome when I came in.

When I spoke, I told the group about my teaching that morning. I led a regular support group for physician interns (a time to share over lunch whatever was on their minds about the experience of being a physician). That day, a young man who had not spoken before shared that his wife had been diagnosed with stomach cancer, and he was trying to be there for her while fulfilling the grueling schedule of an intern. He lived an hour's drive away and had almost fallen asleep several times on the commute to the hospital. He was soft-spoken and apologetic. Not one of his classmates had known this. Many asked him how they could help and said they would take call for him if he needed. This is unheard of in the life of an intern, already overfilled and sleep deprived. I was moved to tears by his colleagues' show of support and by his sharing.

I admitted to the assembled group that I had weighed the option to cancel that morning's teaching so I could take an earlier plane, as I hated to risk being late. But then I was glad I had stayed. I hoped they understood.

The continued surprise:

Parker chose me to be one of the people he mentored in his home for the next two years. It set me on the course to live an undivided life—not all at once, yet that was the unstoppable turn, the seeing I could never "unsee." It changed my work and my life forever.

DARCY AT-HOME
What surprise has saved you? Made you?

The cold, early morning breeze swept across the pool deck, raising the goose bumps even further on my bare arms and legs. This was my first official Red Cross swimming lesson. A standard and widespread activity in my cohort growing up in the 1960s and '70s. I was in the Beginners class, naturally, and was anxious about what was to come. I had nearly drowned two years prior, chasing my sister into overly deep waters in a nearby lake. Those demons had not been entirely exorcised. I had a tentative relationship with water, especially this water. The prospect of getting into an Olympic-sized pool that was barely heated was grim, especially with a vanishingly small shallow end that I could stand up in to keep my head above water. I was a small, skinny kid with minimal insulation and height. We would be venturing into deeper water eventually, maybe even today. I shivered some more.

The weeks wore on. I never got warm, but I did pass the Beginners course, barely. My reward was a small, square cloth Beginners badge that could be sewn onto your swimsuit. I declined that affectation. A Beginners badge was nothing to crow about.

Fast forward a couple of years, and many hours spent in the water (in that same Olympic pool) with my friends had washed away lingering anxieties. My strength and confidence had grown. Everybody I knew was continuing their Red Cross journey, so I signed up too. After careful consideration, I elected to take the next level up, Juniors. Many of my friends were taking an even higher level, Intermediate, and I knew I was as strong a swimmer as they were. But I still *just* took Juniors. I was too afraid of the repeat humiliation of barely passing Beginners. After the first day in Juniors, I regretted that choice. It was too easy. It didn't challenge me. The surprise was that I didn't know myself. The surprise was that easy was bad, and challenge and uncertainty were good. The surprise was that disappointment in myself was a lot worse than someone else's disappointment in me.

These surprises were my first lesson in self-awareness. They forever changed me. I vowed to never again choose the easy way. To not choose something that would genuinely challenge me to achieve something or better myself felt deeply wrong. I discovered that I had a strongly held value and expectation about gifts and abilities. Whatever you have, you're obligated to use it to better yourself and your community. I honestly don't know where that came from other than observing my parents always working hard.

That boyhood promise to myself has never been broken. I have at times suffered for that vow and made others suffer. I have failed and I have succeeded. I have used my gifts, developed my abilities, and hopefully, in the process, become a better human being and helped others in a meaningful way. The surprise that led to a promise was a thread I picked up as a boy that I've never let go of.

ENDNOTE

The right question is like the key to Tutankhamen's pyramid. It unlocks treasures of memory and story. It invites, even demands, narrative sense-making. "What surprise has saved you, made you?" was such a question. It called for a significant event. It recalled for each of us pivotal moments that unfolded into a lifetime path. No simple surprise would do here; no "time

I touched a hot stove" or "that day I ran into an old friend." The phrases "saved you, made you" required a deeper dive. Asking a powerful question is an art and a practice. We were grateful to adopt this question from Pádraig Ó Tuama.

The events we described came at the right moments in our lives. It brings to mind the quote by Lao Tzu in the *Tao Te Ching*, "When the student is ready, the teacher will appear." When Penny met Parker Palmer, she was primed to hear his words about living an undivided life as a call to follow. Darcy was able to hear his own inner teacher for the first time and was open to take heed. In each of our stories, a single event met something inside us that shaped the course of future discernments, decisions, and behaviors. The power of the question helped us describe discoveries from the core of our being.

We couldn't have taken up a question like this on week one of writing together. Since then, we had been on an odyssey to make coherent sense of our lives, perhaps without quite realizing it. When we wrote the stories in this chapter, we were almost at the end of our writing year. After months of practicing our craft, we had developed more comfort with our own writing and an unquestioned trust in the process and in each other. We had already shared many glimpses into our lives, glimpses that touched upon core aspects of our journeys to knowing and becoming our authentic selves. Now, we were uniquely receptive to the power of this writing prompt. Our time of preparing the soil promoted the depth of story-weaving and meaning-making we describe here.

This was emotional, even raw writing that was meaningful for both of us. It was an act of courage and a welcome gift to share. We sensed we were doing some of our best work and looked forward to what would come next.

> . . . after the long season of tending and growth,
> the harvest comes.

Marge Piercy from "The Seven of Pentacles"

CHAPTER TWELVE

Seeing and Being Seen

SANCTUARY

Suppose it's easy to slip
    into another's green skin,
Bury yourself in leaves

and wait for a breaking,
    a breaking open, a breaking
out. I have, before, been

tricked into believing
    I could be both an I
and the world. The great eye

of the world is both gaze
    and gloss. To be swallowed
by being seen. A dream.

To be made whole
    by being not a witness
but witnessed.

Ada Limón

"Slip into another's green skin," "bury yourself," "breaking open," "breaking out," "witnessed"—the words of Ada Limón's poem swirled around us. They called forth images of nature's froth and ferment—how it adapts, transforms, and feels its way forward, offering up metaphorical mirrors to the evolution in our own lives.

There is tension here, and predictably, a paradox underpins it. On one side there is the urge to keep hidden, safe, buried in leaves, or well camouflaged. Like the snowshoe hare who turns white in the winter from its rusty brown summer color. It blends so well into the snowy landscape it becomes almost invisible until it moves, and sooner or later, move it must. If you are still enough, you'll witness it.

On the other side of the paradox is the need to be seen, to be witnessed in all our largeness and splendor. Nature provides abundant examples. The male Wilson's bird-of-paradise is a sparrow-sized bird boasting bright red plumage on its back, a yellow neck patch, and an electric blue featherless crown combined with characteristic sickle-shaped tail feathers on each side. This over-the-top display is key to attracting the attention of females and to propagation of the species. In other words, critical for survival. Even if we don't have resplendent plumage and tail feathers, we all need to be witnessed by someone or something who can see our wholeness and reflect that back to us.

The final piece of the paradox is the shift from witness to being witnessed, the act of breaking open and out. Again, nature shows the way. Butterflies in their life journey from egg to larva (caterpillar) to pupa to full-fledged winged marvels are a breathtaking example of the scale and breadth that transformation from obscurity to visibility can take. A common and perhaps cliched metaphor for the potential of human growth and development, but a powerful one nonetheless.

Ada Limón's evocative poem "Sanctuary" and the writing prompts that arose opened a window to the impact of seeing and being seen. Rich language provided fertile ground for ideas. For our online writing, the last stanza, "To be made whole by being not a witness but witnessed" almost wrote itself into a prompt. We are eager to share the colors and layers that showed up for us in the stories that follow.

PENNY ONLINE
How have you come to know yourself by being witnessed?

Maybe that is why I love and feel so at home in the deciduous woodlands of the Northeast coast. Not only is this habitat familiar to me, but I am familiar to it. Hundreds of memories—sense memories—come back to populate this thought.

When I was conducting my study of birds as a doctoral student, I focused my work in a 20-acre piece of woods in Maryland. I walked those woods daily, in the spring and summer, for two years. I knew every turn. I felt I could anticipate every newly minted spider web brushing my face in the early mornings. My eyes rested on the grand old oaks and maples, and the younger saplings only 10 or 20 years into their lives. And there was I, at 25, feeling my way into my life. My ears were attuned to the birdsongs so that I could find and follow the Red-eyed Vireo males, stars of my quest. I loved being alone in those woods because I wasn't. I never felt alone, only a small being trying to make sense of all the other beings—the winged kind, the leafed kind. But was I witnessed?

Who really knew me in those years? Who really saw me?

No, it is not true to say I felt witnessed then. That came later when I realized I needed to connect with others. I felt I belonged in the woods—always—but I didn't feel seen, simply held. The same was true in the woodlands of my childhood. I made a place mine by exploring every part of it again and again—the old Douglas Estate with its grand trees and fields of daffodils gone wild and the planted formal gardens. Me, a 10-year-old, befriending every path, every subtlety. I was befriended in return by the feeling of being home and at home. An eagle flying over would have seen a happy little girl taking in the beauty and wonder all by herself. Comfortable in her own skin.

ON REFLECTION . . .

PENNY
Fast Forward to Now

When I turned 80, two dear friends hosted a one-hour online Zoom party for me. They suggested I invite up to 30 people and that each would have a few minutes to share a brief memory or story.

It was a joy to invite dear ones from many parts of my life—family, colleagues, friends, mentors, as well as some whom I'd taught—partners in life and in work.

During that emotion-filled hour, I let myself be bathed in an unimaginable outpouring of love. Love was the common denominator. My computer screen showed 32 tiny squares filled with the smiling, laughing, loving faces of people who are dear to me. I don't remember many of the words they said, but it wasn't about words. I felt seen and known. My friends knew I loved them, and I felt their love in return. I was bathed in the joy that came from our years of walking together through our lives, or whatever part each shared.

A body can't go through that kind of experience very often. It is almost too painful to let in such an outpouring of affection and affirmation. Yet I did let it in. It was a priceless gift. It named in a new way what my life story is about. Without fully realizing it, I have built a life of connections, letting myself be seen, known, and loved as I have witnessed, known, and loved others. I could not wish for anything better.

DARCY ONLINE
How have you come to know yourself by being witnessed?

I couldn't control the pain. This young collie had a rapidly moving, highly fatal infection. It was ascending the front leg and would soon get to the tissues around the shoulder and adjacent chest. The medical name is necrotizing fasciitis (also known as flesh-eating disease). It's caused by a Streptococcal bacteria and often requires amputation and/or aggressive tissue debridement and drainage, plus antibiotics and intensive care. It was the first time I'd confronted this disease face to face.

The last injection of a potent opioid painkiller had not worked to reduce the dog's pain. The dog lay on its side in the cage next to us. Heavily sedated from the drug but still whimpering and whining. I turned to the owner to discuss next steps. Tears filled her eyes. The prospect of putting her dog through aggressive surgery (maybe multiple), many days in intensive care, and with a less-than-certain outcome was more than she could imagine. She decided to let go, say goodbye, and not pursue further treatment. The suffering was too much.

As we stood beside the cage facing each other after her whispered, tear-filled decision, she stepped forward and hugged me. It took me by surprise. I had never before been hugged by a client. After my initial shock, I teared up. When she stepped back, tears now streaming down her face, the full impact landed on me. I had never been seen this way by a client before. This was one human being sharing her pain with another. Human to human. Not as a family member, not as a friend or close partner. Just two human beings who met a couple of hours ago, but both immersed in a river of lost hope. Hugged in the same way we've held each other over the millennia in times of grief and loss.

Never had I felt so deeply witnessed and seen as a human being, not just as a veterinarian. This was an invitation to view and know my own humanity, to open to it and to carry it forward. It made me a better person, and a better veterinarian and caregiver. My heart is filled with gratitude.

ON REFLECTION . . .

DARCY
Fast Forward to Now

I turned 65 this year. I don't know what 65 is supposed to feel like, but I get messages from the government about pensions and old age security, so in the view of society, I have entered a new phase. Although I don't care about the number that is my age, I have to agree that I've come to a different time in life. I've changed lanes into one that's a bit slower, more considered, more curated to make space to see clearly and spend what time remains attending to the care and feeding of one's heart and soul and those of others.

I've been worn into who I've become. There is a delightful acceptance and acknowledgment that the world is a provocative and fascinating endeavor that I have, with gratitude, found a place in. There is much I don't understand and never will, but I'll keep looking, keep wondering, keep being amazed, keep honoring, keep being witnessed, and bearing witness to what has passed and what may come.

MORE TO SAY

Like our online writing prompt, the poem's first line, "Suppose it's easy to slip into another's green skin . . ." pretty much handed the at-home prompt to us on a platter. It turned out to be a powerful one for both of us, even though we came at it from very different perspectives. After we wrote the stories and read them to one another the following week, there seemed to be an afterglow about them that called us to say more about the experience of writing them.

In this section, then, we'd like to show you our real-time responses to that writing—we've labeled it "What We Each Thought." In its way, you can see another view into our Writing Together process: the kind of conversations we had and affirmations we gave to each other. We hope you'll find them interesting and instructive.

PENNY AT-HOME
If you could slip into the skin of an "other," who would it be? What would it be like?

You died way too soon, far too young, at 51. And so I never got to ask you what it was like being you; what it felt like as your fingers flew over the keys, hour upon hour, practicing and per-fecting the beauty of a Bach fugue, a Beethoven sonata, or the endless Czerny exercises to keep your fingers supple. What was it like to love my father so completely that you were will-ing to give your whole life over to being with him almost all day every day? From the outside it looked so idyllic—always hug-ging in the kitchen, cooking, practicing the piano right across the hallway from where he was painting—all day, every day.

You even told me once that you wished you lived in Israel in a kibbutz so my sister and I could be taken care of and give you more freedom. I was shocked. Still, I felt your love. I felt your loneliness.

I feel you now—the making do with never enough money. Yet the laughter and good food (your favorites: shepherd pie, chicken cacciatore), always stretching the few dollars to make them last. You had to feel ashamed and angry at yourself that you told me not to bring a friend home for dinner one time, as we couldn't afford it. You hid the angst, but you didn't. You felt sick all the time—you said you had not been pain-free since you were 16. What was life supposed to give? Did you know how loving and loved you were?

You fainted often. Your heart held the stress. You were a loved but caged bird, needing to fly even as you made a home of your cage.

I did try on, slip into, your skin. I ate you whole—I felt your self-judgment, your competence, your giving in to customs even as you dared to be yourself. I felt your body weaken, sicken, and die too soon. I broke free to be my own body, follow my own lights—be NOT who you were (infirm, weak, giving without claiming your own needs for friends), to stretch for more. You wanted me to have that yellow dress, and you bought it for me even though you couldn't afford it. How did you do that? The why is easy—you saw my need and everything in you wanted to give it to me. You wanted to be there for me in a way no one was there for you. You wanted me to be there for you in a way I was too young for—too much a child, your child, to be able to be a witness to your spoken griefs. You felt trapped. I couldn't be the friend you needed; I was only 13. I couldn't help.

Your fingers opened your heart to the greater vistas of all that music—music saved you. You taught children and adults to play the piano with feeling. Everyone fell in love with you. You were beautiful and giving and fiercely committed to excellence. You didn't hold back when it came to playing the piano—you were a truth teller in service of what the music called for. You were patient with your laggards, me among them.

What dreams did you have that slowly faded? To be a concert pianist? To have luxury and comfort? (You fell in love? I'm making this up, but know the outline: an affair, a wealthy man who gave you expensive gifts and came once to our house—to the door, only). You couldn't do it. You said, to my sister, it was for us. You couldn't leave us.

Life isn't straightforward. More than one thing can be true at the same time. You don't know, you didn't know, how long you had. You filled the world with your being for every one of your moments. You didn't hide, even if you thought you did. And you were so smart, emotionally and intellectually smart, even if you thought you weren't.

I never wanted to be you. But I wanted to know you. I still do.

WHAT WE EACH THOUGHT

PENNY

This question burrowed to the well of my being and up came a stream of images and memories I didn't know were awaiting release—memories that made me sad, made me glad. I did know my mother after all—more than I had imagined. I knew the pain and gifts she carried, and her beauty, at least from my child's view. I felt I captured something of her that spoke of heartache and sadness, mine and hers. When Darcy teared up in hearing my writing, it brought the added poignancy of being witnessed—and for having brought my mother to life in a way that could touch another.

DARCY

Such a powerful imagining of joys and struggles. A mother gone too soon with no opportunity to be known in a fuller way by a daughter. A longing left hanging. It deeply moved me and yes, I teared up. All I could do was put my hand on my heart, as I was too choked up to speak.

DARCY AT-HOME
If you could slip into the skin of an "other" who would it be? What would it be like?

I've mulled it over long enough, so I'll just say it. I would like to step into the skin of a goat. One might be perplexed by my choice. Granted, there are a lot of other animals I could have chosen that are more beautiful, dramatic, or symbolic. Why not a tiger, elephant, or an owl? A fair question.

There is something about goats that draws me in. It's not their modest size or that you can get your arms around them (handy for veterinary work). They are not overly attractive, although baby goats (or kids) are devastatingly cute. The most familiar goats are domesticated species that have been of great use to mankind over hundreds of years, supplying meat, milk, and fiber. I respect what they have given to human societies, but that's not the source of my interest. It's in their eyes. Admittedly, their eyes can be off-putting with their horizontal pupils, but that strangeness passes as you look more inquisitively. If you take a moment and concentrate, then you see something else, and it's looking right back at you with the same curious gaze. There is intelligence and a personality there.

So, throw me into a goat's body just to see how it fits and feels. Oh, and please make it a Nubian goat, who characteristically have big, floppy ears. I've had the lifelong pleasure of big saucer-like ears stuck solidly in place. I'd like to try some big, floppy ones for a change so that I can flick them around in dramatic fashion.

What I'm particularly curious about is the inner lives of goats. What constitutes a good day for them (other than eating, for which they have a prodigious and willing capacity to eat almost anything)? What are they thinking about? Are they consumed with soulful musings about who they are and why they exist? What do they think about us, or other species? I suspect that goats have strong opinions about most things and that pragmatism and not-suffering-fools-gladly heavily influence the positions they take. Buttressing this is a wisdom and clear-eyed understanding of the reality of the world.

After getting to know my herd mates, I would tenderly, and with compassion, ask what they hope and wish for. This is an uncomfortable question for a faux goat to be asking. As interesting and important as goats are, they are not an apex species. They are flight animals. Like other herbivores, they run away from threats to live and eat another day. Obstreperous billy goats notwithstanding. Tomorrow they could end up on someone's plate, be chased by dogs, or graze peacefully in a pasture. How do they hold this vulnerability, this fear, this pervasive uncertainty? How would they judge their keepers? I'm not sure I would like what they have to say about the latter.

I will of course never know the answers to these questions. All I really know is that there is someone behind those eyes looking back at me. Maybe wondering what my hopes, dreams, and intentions are. Perhaps goats in their way are asking more of me. Inviting me to thoughtfully consider where I sit in the kingdom of animals and what my duties and responsibilities should be to my kin. Maybe they are hoping that I'll see myself as part of everything that moves and breathes. Not separate from. Not an individual. Not above or below. No dominion over. Just one of them and one of us, all trying to get by and do our best, one day at a time.

WHAT WE EACH THOUGHT

DARCY

This was fun to write. Many times, I've wondered what it would be like to slip into, and fully inhabit, the skin of an animal. To feel their bodies, their athleticism and power, to see what they see, to hear what they hear, and to sample the bursting and unimaginable array of smells they sense. This is very Dr. Dolittle, but I would so love to communicate with animals in a direct way (beyond the nonverbal ways we currently use). It would have been so helpful to have a thoughtful conversation with my dog and cat patients. All this is another way of saying I would like to slip into the spirit of an animal. To feel their wholeness and how they deeply inhabit the present moment and their spirit-filled bodies.

PENNY

One of the great pleasures of this year of writing with Darcy was to experience his depth of knowledge, delight, and respect for all living beings—especially four-footed ones! This goat came alive for me in the detailed and expressive way only a keen and empathic observer and healer of animals could depict. I laughed out loud at the charm of his writing and his playful comparison of ears—his and his Nubian goat's. He said he had fun writing it, and I had fun listening to him read it!

ENDNOTE: THE GIFTS OF SEEING AND BEING SEEN

We never knew in advance what approach each of us would take to our writing topics. At times there was remarkable symmetry of subject and depth (e.g., think back to chapter 3 and our forays into love and loneliness). Here, we diverged dramatically in our "take" on the question. Darcy was playful, imagining himself as a goat. Penny was wistful, imagining herself as her mother.

We always appreciated each other's writing, whatever came. In fact, it was a benchmark of our year. Similarities showed our kindredness. Yet perhaps it was our delight in our differences that was even more impactful. Being wholly affirmed in our uniqueness helped us bring more of ourselves into our writing. Such wholehearted encouragement to show up fully gave us increasing courage to express ourselves more freely, with less caution. In this welcoming space, we came to anticipate reading aloud what we had committed to the page. It was a powerful cycle: writing to know ourselves better, wanting to be known by each other, disclosing ever more gradations of who we are, sharing out loud, being warmly received. Repeat.

On this day, unexpectedly, we revealed more of ourselves by "seeing the other" with our hearts. We are defined in part by what we observe, what moves us, what we pay attention to, whether it be the particularity of place, the essence and spirit of animals, or our profound connection with loved ones. And by putting ourselves in someone else's skin, who we are, at essence, was also made visible. Yes, the "other" was revealed, but so were we. It is a case in point of "seeing and being seen!"

No one can ever fully know another—that is the beautiful mystery of being. Yet, as we have learned throughout our year of writing together, when we dare to show up whole, it makes us more trustworthy, accessible, knowable. And it makes us more lovable.

It is only with the heart that one can see rightly;
what is essential is invisible to the eye.

—Antoine de Saint-Exupéry

CHAPTER THIRTEEN

Inner Light

There's a dark so deep beneath the sea the creatures beget their own light. This feat, this act of adaptation, I could say, is beautiful

Paul Tran from "Bioluminescence"

Things that glow in the dark, especially animals that glow. How extraordinary is that! Bioluminescence is a natural phenomenon that shows up mostly in marine animals. From microscopic dinoflagellates (plankton) and bacteria to larger animals like jellyfish and deep-sea creatures such as vampire squid and anglerfish, nature can out-imagine any of us. Just stroll through a picture gallery of the bizarre, otherworldly life forms living in the ink-black ocean depths. It's the stuff of science fiction and fantasy. And yet, there is light.

The light comes from a chemical reaction, most often involving a substance called luciferin. When broken down by the enzyme luciferase, light is emitted. An interesting name for a molecule. Luciferin evokes Lucifer, the devil, fire, and Hell. However, the Latin derivation for Lucifer is "light bearer." A humbling example of how our perceptions, associations, and experiences can take us away from original meanings, sources, and truths.

Coming back to meanings. Bioluminescence. What a word! This six-syllable lovely has an ascending triumphal cadence and slips off the tongue with definitive hiss. *Bios* is Greek for life. *Lumen* is Latin for light. Life light! It does not get much better than that for a provocative writing prompt and one that was compellingly reinforced by the first lines of Paul Tran's poem highlighted at the beginning of the chapter. The idea of a guiding light in the darkness is a spiritual signpost that shows up in almost all wisdom traditions. That symbolism was embedded in us too, and we came back to it for our at-home writing prompt.

The last line of "Bioluminescence" talked about approaching the bottom of the sea that wasn't the bottom. It invited us to think about not seeing clearly or holding onto what we thought was a truth that turned out not to be so. Our online writing prompt emerged from those wonderings: "What did you have to forfeit or shed to see the truer world?"

We wrote for 10 minutes online (it felt right that day). The stories were brief and yet started us down a fork into darker woods that we continued to follow with our at-home writing. We've included them to show how short some of the online pieces were. They were another example of how our online writing was the initial on-ramp to what came next in our at-home efforts, the warmup before the main event.

PENNY ONLINE
What did you have to forfeit or shed to see the truer world?

I thought it would be so much easier if I could fit into a structure already laid out—an easy road to acceptance and success. Academic medicine is where I landed, and I strove to fit the mold. I was out of my element yet felt I could work hard and ultimately become what that world expected: a three-legged stool—doing research, being a clinician, and teaching. Two of the three legs suited me; research, not so much. Why do I hate rules and yet long to be successful in following them?

Perhaps the miracle of my inner resistance is that I simply could not become something I wasn't. I loved parts of that world yet felt squeezed into a shape that wasn't me. I had to forfeit being a great academic to find my way to give my true gifts. I had to leave the organized part of that world to invite others to explore their own truths.

By acknowledging to myself and others the vulnerability I felt, I opened windows, doors, let in light. It started when I asked others to share their truths and made a safe place for them to do so. I did it for others who were more suited to stay in that world, yet with deep needs to be seen and known. Ultimately that wasn't my home. My home was finding fellow journeyers and inviting others to join us.

I let go of being what the system demanded and found my way.

PENNY

This brief reflection seemed more like a précis, a beginning, rather than a full telling. Sometimes our online writing was like that. It opened a topic just a crack, gave a hint of what might follow. Nothing is lost. Sometimes a theme appears as a barely sketched storyline to be picked up later, often unconsciously, at a different time. Or perhaps this 10-minute writing was a continuation.

Again and again during the year, I found myself returning to the theme of being true to myself, of finding my authentic path, trying and failing to force-fit myself, listening to my inner voice when I was off track, and ultimately finding and staying on a road to which I belonged, that was mine to travel.

I realize now that this week's online writing was in fact a summary of sorts that linked together and made meaning of many of my earlier reflections. It's as if my brain had been working beneath my conscious awareness to knit together a coherent story from the many pieces I've remembered.

Perhaps there is such a thing as an organizing theme of one's life, set in motion early on and replayed with variations along the road to discovering and becoming one's best self. Or perhaps this set of stories allowed me to find and revisit one recurring theme on my life's path. Perhaps there are others awaiting discovery.

DARCY ONLINE
What did you have to forfeit or shed to see the truer world?

I had to forfeit the idea, much treasured and burnished, that I would not change. By the time I was in my early twenties, university behind me, an interesting career ahead, and in a stable relationship, I thought, okay, this is it. I know who and what I am. I understand how the world works, I have a plan, and the road looks clear and open. Excellent! Full speed ahead. Such hubris. It worked well for a time. That open road became strewn with the fallen branches of hopes and dreams and littered with potholes of regret and disappointment. Dark clouds loomed, threatening rain. Threatening something.

It was not one big crash or barrier breached. Rather, it was many small bumps. Too many euthanasias, too much suffering and loss, unresolved grief, hoped-for things that didn't happen, and small and not-so-small regrets. The questions "Why?" and "What for?" started creeping in. Unwanted house guests that made a mess and didn't clean up after themselves. They left their crap all over the place and now I had to pick it all up.

It wasn't easy seeing the dark places in the world because they opened dark places within me. I admit, it pissed me off. Anger that the world didn't work the way I thought and fear that I had to change, deeply change, because the world sure wasn't going to. I eventually got to the other side of anger and fear, mostly. To a state of hopeful balance holding those things (in me and in the world) I can't change and those that I can, mostly.

DARCY

When I reread my online story 12 months later, I could feel the abrasive emotions flowing through it. We did not often frame questions that took us intentionally to dark emotions like anger. That was not the intent with the prompt we created, but I went there. I didn't intend to, but as I framed my response and started to peel back layers, emotions arose. They crept into my pen and onto the paper. Sharp edges and sharp words. The rawness and resentment that was emerging in this story no doubt influenced how I approached our at-home prompt. The pot was now simmering and would start to boil with my at-home writing later in the week.

Responding to the online prompt also made visible something that I was not proud of and can struggle with. Anger. Not full-fledged rage or ranting but a coiled-up, background irritation and impatience. Am I the stereotypical grumpy old guy? Yes, I can be, especially when I'm tired or not feeling well. I hate that. Can you be angry that you're angry? I don't know, but it gives me something else to be annoyed about. Not a good strategy. It helps to write about it, to name it, and to look it in the eye. It keeps the anger, impatience, irritation, or whatever shows up that day in front of me to see it for what it is.

Anger is almost always a secondary emotion. There is some other feeling or need giving it life. For me, I think part of it is the impending losses I know are ahead of me. Most of my life has been lived. I still have many good years ahead (I hope), and I also know that, with time, I will lose all those that I love. I will lose my own health and vitality and die too. That's just so damn hard to hold. It hurts, and it makes me angry. At the same time, there is much joy and beauty in the world. I need to name and see that too. A life's work!

Writing about anger was and is hard. I was reluctant to show my jagged, rougher side to Penny, or frankly, to myself. By this time in our year, however, I knew I could open up that part of me and Penny would receive it as she had for all the other stories I wrote, regardless of the feelings written on the page or that arose in the reading aloud.

WHAT'S INSIDE US

We returned to the imagery of "inner light" for at-home writing: "Think of a time when your inner light guided you out of darkness." The topic took us to painful places that we have never written about. Putting it on paper and sharing it took us to a level of vulnerability that we had not yet touched. It felt like our most moving session of the year.

As in chapter 12, we've included post-story reflections (on what we wrote and heard from each other) about our at-home writing. The experience seemed again to call for more to be said. To not only absorb what we'd written but to discern what it meant. To understand and feel the new ground we now walked on.

PENNY AT-HOME
Think of a time when your inner light guided you out of darkness.

There have been times when it was hard to believe I had an inner light, it was a flame so tiny, so small, almost invisible. Mostly I am a sunny, optimistic person who feels the bright wonder of life—but not always.

An experience that comes to mind was one of darkness and confusion. I was helping to develop and lead a wonderful organization that I was involved in from its inception. I believed in our cause and felt aligned with our work: helping physicians to be more human, skillful, and openhearted with their patients, students, colleagues, and themselves. This was what I had trained and worked towards my whole career. I had found a home and could help build it and live in it. It was a Camelot time. I was the mom of this growing endeavor. The world was bright with our passion and the belief in our capacity to fill this huge need.

We were offering multiple courses each year and reaching a growing number of clinicians who were hungry to reconnect their hearts with their work and wide open to learn and deepen their capacity within the trustworthy settings we created. I began as a facilitator of courses and then moved into the role of organization leader, also still teaching and much more.

But all was not well. There were toxic factors at play. I felt a hidden imperative not to change, tweak, or create anything new without explicit permission. Secrets and lack of transparency seemed the rule behind the scenes, while to the world we presented only harmony and invitation. I so believed in the work that I tried to shield others from the unseen toxicity. Wonderful new ideas were quashed before seeing the light of day. I kept going. I felt like a puppet being manipulated by someone else pulling the strings. I wasn't being true to myself, and my light began to extinguish. I sank into a clinical depression, pretending all was well to the outside world while dying on the inside. I thought that the work and our mission mattered more than my mental state. To say it another way, I thought I could bear my mental state in service of the work. But it was too costly.

The tiny flame inside me that couldn't be extinguished demanded attention. I wrestled with the realization that I did not want to die (figuratively or actually), that damping down my light was too high a price to pay for anyone or anything, even a noble cause—especially a noble cause. I had help from supportive friends and a therapist, yet ultimately, I had to face my demons alone: the ones that told me it was my fault, my problem to fix, or my weakness to overcome. Once I faced that reality, I couldn't turn away from it. I wrote a letter resigning from the organization—my community, my home, my passion—and chose my life. I did it well and honorably, and I set myself free.

I had kept unhealthful secrets far too long. I almost disappeared. But I didn't. My inner light guided me back to fullness and to the powerful truth that living anything less than an undivided life was too high a price to pay. It saved the core of me that laughs and creates and loves and can stand up and say "Not This" and "YES."

WHAT WE EACH THOUGHT

PENNY

It is always a surprise to me what memories a question will spark. The combination of inner light and darkness was a call to write about a profoundly challenging time in my life, one I'd never written about in such an open or vulnerable way. I felt the genuineness of what I wrote and such lightness in having it "out." It is no accident that we were a full year into our practice when I wrote this piece. By then, I felt "opened up" to express my own truth (an immense step) and full trust in Darcy to receive it without judgment and with affirmation for me as a person worthy of his friendship and respect. Sharing with a friend over our writing year lifted the stigma, the fear I used to feel in committing my experiences to paper. I have come to realize that my life—full of complexities, successes, failures, embarrassments, and joys—is just a life like any other. I can bear to share it.

DARCY

I was humbled to bear witness to the struggle and tremendous courage that Penny showed. No small thing to step away from your Camelot. Such an inspiring story of coming home to who you are.

DARCY AT-HOME
Think of a time when your inner light guided you out of darkness.

I turned around. I'm not sure what made me do it, but I had had enough of running. Maybe rage had built up enough to overcome fear. Flight, fight, or freeze. These are the survival responses on offer by our brain's hardwired ancient limbic system. The wheel of fortune had spun and with a final sharp click, landed on "fight." I stopped and turned.

This wasn't the first time I had encountered these wolves. Impressive specimens of *Canis lupus* pursued me. Tall and muscular in their grey/black-flecked coats with their golden eyes riveted on me. Small clouds of misted breath burst from their nostrils in the cold air as they huffed and grunted in anticipation of the chase. The group vibrated with primal energy, shifting, dancing, pawing the ground, waiting for the leader to signal that it was time to hunt, to feed. It was a well-oiled pack. Practiced, disciplined, and methodical in their predatory choreography. They knew that, and I knew that.

It was always dark when they emerged, well into night's passage when life flows are at a low ebb for daytime creatures. I rarely saw them, but I knew they were there. I could feel them and their malevolent intent. Tingling fear crept up my spine and paralyzed my muscles. I would start to run. Limbs so heavy I could hardly move. Why can't I move faster? It was like trying to run through waist-deep snow. Just as they were about to make their killing pounce, I would wake up. Heart pounding with a thin layer of chilling sweat covering my boyhood body.

When I was six to eight years old, I had frequent night terrors. Waking up in the still blackness to grapple with the monsters under my bed or the gorilla hiding behind my dresser. Countless nights I'd wake up and shuffle into either my older sister's or parents' bedroom hoping to sleep the rest of the night with them. Most of the time they acquiesced, but not always.

After a string of many middle-of-the-night awakenings, my father surged out of bed and grabbed the back of my neck and marched me to the back door. He flung the door open, pushed me outside and held me there. He repeatedly yelled at me that I had a choice. Either sleep in my own bed or stay outside for the night. Amidst my screaming, that my sister still remembers to this day, I chose my own bed. The lesser of the two bad options. The wolves would have a harder time getting to me in my bed versus the backyard, or so I thought.

Sometime later I met the wolves again. This time I had had enough. After beginning to run, I stopped, turned, and roared at them. No words, just a fist clenched, feral, body-shaking roar. A final life-or-death challenge delivered in the midst of a blinding light. My mind screamed, "This is where I begin and you end. Do your worst. This stops now!"

The night terrors went away shortly thereafter. The blinding inner light that showed up as I turned to face the wolves told me something I had not heard before. It said that I had worth and that I deserved to be here. Come hell or high water, I had value and gifts to give the world. As days turned into years that rolled into decades, that light has stayed within me. Admittedly, it has sputtered occasionally, but mostly, it's been a steady, low, irrepressible glow. It whispers to me in the darkness. Always there. Always felt. Always visible when I take the time to see it.

WHAT WE EACH THOUGHT

DARCY

As I started to ponder inner light, this story sprung forth. Much like the soon-to-pounce wolves I wrote about. Looking back, this experience no doubt shaped the subsequent relationship I had with my father. Thereafter, I mentally kept him at arm's length. Trust had been broken. As I noted in chapter 11, we had a rocky relationship in my adolescent and teenage years that later mellowed.

Ten years after he passed, my father started showing up regularly in my dreams. Nothing dramatic, just us doing mundane things together. Taking road trips and doing chores around the family home. I realized that somehow and at some point, I had forgiven his past transgressions, and as a result, he rejoined my life in an unexpected way. I now see and appreciate my whole father. His struggles and his joy. His darkness and his light. I miss him.

PENNY

It was gripping to read this. It was even more compelling to hear Darcy read his story aloud. I felt it viscerally. It was hard to hear, yet a profound gift to be trusted at this level with his powerful, painful memories and fierce turn to courage. In the midst of him describing boyhood terrors, I am affected by Darcy's deep knowledge and articulate description of the wolves in all their ferocious wildness. It is a sacred act to witness another human being.

ENDNOTE

This was the final writing session of our year-long writing journey. With some amazement, trepidation, and courage, we committed our most vulnerable stories to paper. We each felt the drive to do so before it was too late, recognizing the rare combination of gift and fleeting opportunity to share these painful events, these formative moments, in the safe harbor of our trustworthy space.

We reflected, later, that this writing was a mark of overcoming long-held fears to speak of such pivotal painful times. To write derisive, hurtful things about an important person in one's life is not easy—to admit the destructive impact of a loved father, a visionary boss. Yet the truth-teller in each of us allowed, even propelled us, to walk into our fear and free ourselves by naming it.

It took us a whole year to write about something that had this hold on us, that we had avoided even talking about. It was, we agreed with some awe, a perfect capstone to our year.

Once again, we didn't know we would write these stories when we picked "inner light," and once again, our wiser inner teachers knew this was the time. We had tested the waters with glimpses and hints in earlier chapters. This was the time to share the full story. For each of us.

We felt an unexpected sense of gratitude and release. Freeing oneself from the grip of pain is a milestone on the long road to becoming oneself. Hearing ourselves in the writing, telling, and being received made it human, rendered it acceptable and right-sized. Because we were able to do this, we stand now in a new place in our lives. And, by great good fortune, we are still not finished, still a work in progress with more to come.

CHAPTER FOURTEEN

Walking Through the Door

**PROSPECTIVE IMMIGRANTS
PLEASE NOTE**

Either you will
go through this door
or you will not go through.

If you go through,
there is always the risk
of remembering your name.

Things look at you doubly
and you must look back
and let them happen.

If you do not go through
it is possible
to live worthily

to maintain your attitudes
to hold your position
to die bravely

but much will blind you,
much will evade you,
at what cost who knows?

The door itself
makes no promises.
It is only a door.

Adrienne Rich

In ways both hoped for yet unexpected, our year of writing together opened a door into our lives and into a trustworthy process for writing with a friend over time. We created a path that contained both mystery and known structures for sharing memoir, making more coherent meaning of our lives, and deepening our friendship. We wrote this book for you, our readers, with the hope it would give you inspiration and guidance to embark on your own writing adventure.

We share our closing reflections on each aspect of our year: writing together, meaning-making, and friendship. You might want to consider your own year-end reflections when you come to that time.

WRITING TOGETHER

During our year of writing, early hesitation morphed into a state of ease and acceptance. We felt an increased openness and interest in what would emerge on the page and a growing confidence in our capacity to write and the desire to do so. We discovered that we had more than a few stories to tell, many of them rising from long-forgotten experiences.

Recently, a friend asked us what one word we would use to describe the weekly work of writing and the subsequent creation of this book. We both said "surprise" almost at the same time. Surprise that we *could* write, surprise about the wide range of topics that arose (some deep and difficult), surprise that our already close friendship got even closer, surprise that by writing we discovered more of who we were, surprise that we found some healing and grace about past challenges, and surprise at the passion that developed as we worked on this project. We are so grateful for the unexpected opportunity that allowed us to immerse ourselves in such a rich, creative endeavor.

It feels like serendipity to have stumbled upon and then walked through this open door. That's partly true, and yet three predictable elements led us here and informed the approach we took. First, we both took one, then another, online writing class given by Natalie Goldberg. Her open-hearted insistence and invitation that you just needed to write and not think too hard about it, reduced our insecurity about writing. As she said in her first book, *Writing Down the Bones*, "Writing practice embraces your whole life and doesn't demand any logical form . . . It's a place you can come to wild and unbridled." We took her words to heart. Over time, as our confidence increased and we plumbed deeper depths, other words from our classes also came true, "Write until the blood runs clear."

Second, as Courage & Renewal facilitators, how we met to write was heavily influenced by our experience leading retreats using the principles and practices of the Courage & Renewal approach as guideposts. Because we imagined our best writing would happen in the same trustworthy space, we naturally included the approach in our Writing Together process. It provided a safe and affirming structure and container that we both knew could hold whatever arose.

Third, we've been close friends for years and have worked on many projects together. We already had a firm foundation of relational trust in place on which to start building something new. All these elements set us up to say yes to the open door, take a risk on what might show up, and step forward with a process we knew we could rely on, come what may.

MEANING-MAKING

Our experiences live in each of us as disparate, loosely connected threads. In the year of our writing together and the additional year to further shape the material for this book, we found ways to weave the varied textures, colors, and patterns of our lives into a coherent tapestry. Responding to different prompts each week gave rise to the form for our book. Rather than telling our life stories from beginning to end, we have shared glimpses into many aspects of our lives and the varied influences upon us.

We did not set out to write our memoirs, yet pieces of memoir emerged. We have had the pleasure of putting into words moments that moved us and the relief of writing hard stories, long kept private. We formed multifaceted pictures through this mix of pivotal events, painful challenges, poignant delights and sadnesses, important conversations, and wordless pleasures. Nothing is ever the "whole story"; still, we felt a profound sense of coming to the right stopping point at year's end.

We find to our surprise that we each feel more complete. We sense that we have created an integrated picture for ourselves (and perhaps for our readers) of who we are as human beings: our giftedness, our fragile places, what we care about, and how we show that caring. It is an amazement to us that this is so. There is a knowing we now carry that our lives, like all lives, have worth and substance. Writing has helped us step more fully into that knowing. We need not have published our writing to feel that knowing.

What does it mean to feel more complete? In writing from our hearts and being witnessed by each other, we found the freedom to let ourselves be known more completely. In doing so, we came to know ourselves better, to see the arc of our lives and to find increased acceptance and gladness for who we have become and are still becoming. We have discovered and revealed pieces that fill in the unwoven parts of our lives. We have been able to put to rest some old hurts and find forgiveness and love in their place, learning again the poignant lesson that there is always the chance to re-examine unresolved or still-painful memories and come to greater peace within oneself. These were unexpected gifts in a year rich with gifts.

FRIENDSHIP

We come to know ourselves and where we belong by what the world reflects back to us. We live in relation to people, place, and time—past, present, and future. One of the safe and sustaining harbors we all need in our travels is a good friend, and if we're lucky, many good friends. Maria Popova has shared ". . . the greatest gift a friend can give is to sing back to you the song of yourself when you forget it." To be known, to be seen, to be heard—it's what we all need. We need that as much as the food we eat. Friendship is the steadying handhold we can grasp to keep us anchored in the here and now. When we forget that, our friends remind us.

"We could have never done this alone" almost became a chorus between us because we said it so often. "This" being the weekly writing and putting it all into a book. It's because we did it together that it happened at all. We showed up, listened, and affirmed each other regardless of the day or how we felt. We wrote because we were friends. Friends first, writing second. The idea of the project germinated between us and was sustained by the strength of our relationship which, as noted earlier, strengthened our friendship even further. A virtuous cycle!

We will be forever changed by the writing we did together. The stories that emerged opened both our hearts and our eyes to the beautiful and sometimes hard world we live in. That this happened as we sat (virtually speaking) beside each other is a wondrous thing.

EMBARKING ON YOUR OWN WRITING JOURNEY

Process is king, or queen! Take your pick, but it's the secret to success in any undertaking, whether it's writing, doing surgery, building a house, or baking bread. Let go of the outcome and trust the process. If the process is sound, the outcome will be as well. We thought carefully about our Writing Together process, tested it, and found that it worked well for us. We hope it will work as well for you too.

Some high points about the process come to mind:

- Find a friend, or friends, and make a commitment to each other to write regularly on a schedule that you agree on. Stick to it.

- Create a trusted space using the Touchstones. This is the heart and soul of holding a generative space for writing, and especially for sharing and affirmation.

- Don't worry about writing good stuff. Natalie Goldberg repeatedly said in her classes, "Write down any old shit, it's practice, it doesn't matter."

- Use "third things" to open up conversations and writing possibilities. We used poetry, but you can choose anything that speaks to you (music, art, nature, etc.).

- Keep the writing tasks manageable. If you are just beginning to write, avoid big, general writing prompts (e.g., "Why do I exist?") or those that take you to tender places that you may not be ready to write about or share. Short, simple questions or prompts that have some specificity are a great place to start (e.g., "A memory of a great meal") or pivot off a provocative word or phrase taken directly from a poem.

In Appendix I, we share the writing prompts and titles of the poems we used in our year of writing. We invite you to use them as written, or modify to suit your needs, or use them as idea starters for you to develop your own unique and compelling prompts. In Appendix II is an additional list of some of our favorite poems used over the years in the retreats we've led.

Every writing journey is different. Whatever you uncover as you embark on your own foray will be the right thing!

So, remember, find a friend (or friends), make a commitment, follow the process, relax and write, and have fun.

THE LAST WORD

This year of writing has given us so much more than we could have known when we started. We trust the Writing Together process will work for you as well as it did for us and that you'll find our stories to be helpful and interesting. Frank Herbert (author of the *Dune* science fiction books) remarked that, "There is no real ending. It's just the place where you stop the story." We'll stop ours here and wholeheartedly invite you to start yours. It's time to pick up your pen, walk through the open door, and join us!

Appendix I

Writing Prompts and Poems Used During Our Writing Together Year

The writing prompts below go to a lot of different places. Some are lighthearted (laughing hard, good meals), some evoke joyful moments (seeing beauty, an experience beyond words), and others go to uncharted waters where you don't know what will arise. As we've mentioned previously, we mainly chose to use Pàdraig Ó Tuama's book *Poetry Unbound: 50 Poems to Open Your World* as our source for poetry.[8] When we started a new writing session, we'd simply turn to another poem in the book.

For each poem, we created a pair of prompts. Listed first is the online one we used while together on Zoom. The second prompt was the at-home writing topic we considered on our own and then sent our work to each other a couple of days before our next online meeting.

Sometimes the at-home prompt built on the online one, while at other times they diverged significantly. This depended on feelings evoked by the poem, particular words or phrases that spoke to us, or how we showed up that day (tired, energetic). We were also influenced by things going on in our lives (sick pets, ill friends, new relationships, recent experiences, travel).

---

8 All poems from our writing year except "Sanctuary" by Ada Limón are from Pádraig Ó Tuama, *Poetry Unbound: 50 Poems to Open Your World*, W. W. Norton & Company, 2023.

If we reread the poems again, no doubt we would come up with different questions/prompts. Like the edge of a Möbius strip, our outer and inner worlds flowed into and out of our writing constantly. **The bolded poems and prompts** with their related stories are the ones included in the book.

If you are so moved, use the prompts below to spark your own writing—or modify them, or create new ones. Either way, pick up your pen or open your laptop and write. Enjoy!

SESSION 1 POEM "Wonder Woman" by Ada Limón
- What myths have I needed and how has myth been a guide?
- What beliefs served you in the past and what beliefs serve you now?

SESSION 2 POEM "Book of Genesis" by Kei Miller
- What silent dreams may be hovering?
- What would it mean to have a full heart?

SESSION 3 POEM "Phase One" by Dilruba Ahmed
- What do you wish to forgive yourself for?
- What has allowed you to turn from smallness to largeness?

SESSION 4 POEM "A Portable Paradise" by Roger Robinson
- What paradise lives in your pocket?
- What would you shine the lamp on like the fresh hope of morning?

SESSION 5 POEM "Worm" by Gail McConnell
- What has so absorbed you that you have changed it and been changed by it?
- When has the depth of knowing and the lightness of being come together for you?

SESSION 6 POEM "Wishing Well" by Gregory Pardlo
- When have you unexpectedly connected with a stranger?
- What encounter with a stranger changed you?

SESSION 7 POEM "All My Friends Are Finding New Beliefs" by Christian Wiman
- What do you find yourself paying attention to in the swirl of life?
- What do you love about speed?

SESSION 8 POEM "Don't Miss Out! Book Right Now for the Journey of a Lifetime!" by Imtiaz Dharker

- When was a time you were left breathless?
- Who or what compels you to go miles and miles to know better?

SESSION 9 POEM **"A Blessing"** by James Wright

- **Describe your sensual memories of a recent time.**
- **When have you held love and loneliness together?**

SESSION 10 POEM **"The Word"** by Zaffar Kunial

- When was a time when you deviated from "the life" and enjoyed it?
- **What are you betwixt and between and what serves as a halfway house?**

SESSION 11 POEM **"Bullshit"** by Vahni (Anthony) Capildeo

- **What word do you like to roll around in your mouth like sweet candy?**
- **Think of an experience that took you beyond words.**

SESSION 12 POEM "Some Things I Like" by Lemn Sissay

- What are some things I like but shouldn't?
- What experience from your past has prepared you for the work you do or have done?

SESSION 13 POEM "Say My Name" by Meleika Gesa-Fatafehi

- Why did you choose the name you did for a dear one?
- Create your own name for something beautiful in your environment. Write about your choice.

SESSION 14 POEM **"Reporting Back to Queen Isabella"** by Lorna Goodison

- Write about an experience of abundance.
- **What role has doing what's expected played in your life?**

SESSION 15 POEM "We Lived Happily during the War" by Ilya Kaminsky

- How do you find your way knowing the immense suffering in the world?
- What matters to you about the way you live?

SESSION 16 POEM   **"Writing the camp"** by Yousif M. Qasmiyeh
- What goes unnoticed that notices you?
- **When did art make something happen for you?** (from Pádraig Ó Tuama's *Poetry Unbound* weekly Substack newsletter, June 4, 2023)

SESSION 17 POEM   "Battlegrounds" by Xochitl-Julisa Bermejo
- Who are the unseen in your life/world you would invite to speak?
- What do you see when you experience this place?

SESSION 18 POEM   "Whereas my eyes land on the shoreline" by Layli Long Soldier
- Where in your life can you be yourself, be true, feel feelings?
- What valuable things took you a long time to learn?

SESSION 19 POEM   "Miami Airport" by Raymond Antrobus
- When have you felt helpless?
- What has anger given and taken away from you?

SESSION 20 POEM   **"reconciliation"** by Jónina Kirton
- What worlds have you bridged?
- **How has "not belonging" been a gift or strength for you?**

SESSION 21 POEM   "All Bread" by Margaret Atwood
- When have you felt a deep connection to what you are eating?
- Describe a place that brings you most alive.

SESSION 22 POEM   "Prayer" by Faisal Mohyuddin
- When is a time you touched into the great mystery?
- How or where do you find yourself in the great mystery?

SESSION 23 POEM   From *The Book of Hours* by Rainer Maria Rilke
- What have you had to let go of to make room for what comes next?
- How have your old failures given rise to white combs and sweet honey?

SESSION 24 POEM "How Prayer Works" by Kaveh Akbar
- What has made you laugh so hard you forgot everything else?
- What do you find worthy of worship?

SESSION 25 POEM "Of Course She Looked Back" by Natalie Diaz
- What has allowed you to find yourself in a time of tragedy?
- Describe a memorable meal and what made it so.

SESSION 26 POEM "After the Goose that Rose like the God of Geese" by Martín Espada
- What truce do you find yourself making with the world?
- What has helped you move from cacophony to quiet in your head?

SESSION 27 POEM **"On Receiving Father at JFK after his Long Flight from Kashmir"** by Rafiq Kathwari
- **A time you were changed by the culture you found yourself in.**
- **A story of holding someone's hand**.

SESSION 28 POEM **"22: La Bota"** by Esteban Rodríguez
- **When do you feel at home on the ground you walk?**
- **When has the presence of absence moved you?**

SESSION 29 POEM "In Leticia's Kitchen Drawer" by Peggy Robles-Alvarado
- What story comes to mind when you look at or touch a treasured object in your house?
- What cold weather story wants to be told?

SESSION 30 POEM **"Song"** by Tracy K. Smith
- **A memory of hands.**
- **What surprise has saved you? Made you?** (from Pádraig Ó Tuama's *Poetry Unbound* weekly newsletter, Substack, November 19, 2023)

SESSION 31 POEM   "The Place Where We Are Right" by Yehuda Amichai
- When was a time when you thought you were right but weren't?
- What is stretching you? (Dec. 4, 2023, follow-up from Natalie Goldberg workshop the preceding days)

SESSION 32 POEM   "What You Missed that Day You Were Absent from Fourth Grade" by Brad Aaron Modlin
- Write about memories of the wind.
- What did "I am" mean to me as a kid and what does it mean to me now?

SESSION 33 POEM   "Consider the Hands that Write this Letter" by Aracelis Girmay
- What do you need to hold still to enable action?
- What do you need both hands to do?

SESSION 34 POEM   "Living in the Past" by Joy Ladin
- Write about not dying of COVID.
- No at-home question this session.

SESSION 35 POEM   **"Sanctuary"** by Ada Limón[9]
- **How have you come to know yourself by being witnessed?**
- **If you could slip into the skin of an "other," who would it be? What would it be like?**

SESSION 36 POEM   **"Bioluminescence"** by Paul Tran
- **What did you have to forfeit or shed to see the truer world?**
- **Think of a time when your inner light guided you out of darkness.**

---

9 Ada Limón, "Sanctuary," from *The Hurting Kind*. Milkweed Editions, 2022.

Appendix II

Additional Poems to Consider

Below are some of our favorite poems (and poets) used over the years of leading retreats. They lend themselves to the creation of compelling questions and writing prompts. Each poem is easily found online by title and author, or in the books listed on the following pages. We encourage you to support the work and legacy of these and other poets.

We have included one or two poems from each poet, at a glance, as an introduction to their work; there are many others to discover! We hope you will enjoy them as much as we do.

AUTHOR	POEM
Wendell Berry	"The Peace of Wild Things" "Our Real Work"
Lucille Clifton	"blessing the boats"
Billy Collins	"Shoveling Snow With Buddha"
Václav Havel	"Hope" (not a poem; oft-quoted passage)
Anne Hillman	"We Look With Uncertainty"
Stanley Kunitz	"The Layers"
Lao Tzu	"Always We Hope"
Denise Levertov	"A Gift" "Of Being"

AUTHOR	POEM
Antonio Machado	"Last Night, As I Was Sleeping"
Mark Nepo	"Crossing Some Ocean In Myself"
	"We Waste So Much Energy"
Pablo Neruda	"All paths lead to the same goal" (from "Towards the Splendid City," Nobel lecture, 1971)
Gunilla Norris	"Paradox of Noise"
Naomi Shihab Nye	"Kindness"
	"Shoulders"
John O'Donohue	"For Celebration"
	"For A New Beginning"
Mary Oliver	"In Blackwater Woods"
	"The Summer Day"
Marge Piercy	"The Seven of Pentacles"
Adrienne Rich	"Prospective Immigrants, Please Note"
Rainer Maria Rilke	"I believe in all that has never yet been spoken"
	"I love the dark hours of my being"
Rumi	"Lame Goat"
	"Sky Circles"
May Sarton	"The Angels and The Furies"
	"Now I Become Myself"
William Stafford	"You, Reading This Be Ready"
Rosemerry Wahtola Trommer	"Watching My Friend Pretend Her Heart Is Not Breaking"
Derek Walcott	"Love After Love"
David Whyte	"Sweet Darkness"
	"Start Close In"

POETRY REFERENCES

"The Peace of Wild Things"—Berry, Wendell. *The Peace of Wild Things*. Penguin Books, 2018.

"Our Real Work"—Berry, Wendell. *Standing By Words*. Shoemaker & Hoard, 1983.

"blessing the boats"—Clifton, Lucille. *Blessing the Boats: New and Selected Poems, 1988–2000*. BOA Edition, Ltd, 2000.

"Shoveling Snow With Buddha"—Collins, Billy. *Sailing Alone Around the Room: New and Selected Poems*. Random House, 2001.

"Hope" (not a poem; oft-quoted passage)—Havel, Václav. *Disturbing the Peace: A Conversation with Karel Huizdala*. (Vintage; Reprint Edition, 1991), 181–182.

"We Look With Uncertainty"—Hillman, Anne. *Awakening the Energies of Love: Discovering Fire for the Second Time*. Bramble Books, 2008.

"The Layers"—Kunitz, Stanley. *The Collected Poems*. W.W. Norton, 2000.

"Always We Hope"—Lao Tzu. In: Le Guin, Ursula K. *Lao Tzu: Tao Te Ching: A Book about the Way and the Power of the Way*. Shambhala; Reissue edition, 2019.

"A Gift"—Levertov, Denise, Paul A. Lacey, and Eavan Boland. *The Collected Poems of Denise Levertov*. New Directions, 2024.

"Of Being"—Levertov, Denise, Paul A. Lacey, and Eavan Boland. *The Collected Poems of Denise Levertov*. New Directions, 2024.

"Last Night, As I Was Sleeping"—Machado, Antonio. *Times Alone: Selected Poems of Antonio Machado*, Translated by Robert Bly. Wesleyan University Press, 1983.

"Crossing Some Ocean In Myself"—Nepo, Mark. *The Way Under the Way: A Place of True Meeting*. Sounds True, 2016.

"We Waste So Much Energy" (Excerpt)—Nepo, Mark. *The Book of Awakenings: Having the Life You Want by Being Present to the Life You Have.* Conari Press, 2000.

"All paths lead to the same goal"—Neruda, Pablo. The Nobel Prize. "Towards the Splendid City," Nobel lecture (Excerpt), 1971. https://www.nobelprize.org/prizes/literature/1971/neruda/lecture.

"Paradox of Noise"—Norris, Gunilla. *Sharing Silence: Meditation Practice and Mindful Living.* Harmony, 1993.

"Kindness"—Shihab Nye, Naomi. Different Ways to Pray. Far Corner Books, 1995.

"Shoulders"—Shihab Nye, Naomi. *Red Suitcase.* BOA Editions Ltd, 1994.

"For Celebration"—O'Donohue, John. *To Bless the Space Between Us: A Book of Blessings.* Convergent Books, 2008.

"For A New Beginning"—O'Donohue, John. *Benedictus: A Book of Blessings.* Bantam Books, 2007.

"In Blackwater Woods"—Oliver, Mary. *New and Selected Poems - Volume One.* Beacon Press, 1992.

"The Summer Day"—Oliver, Mary. *New and Selected Poems - Volume One.* Beacon Press, 1992.

"The Seven of Pentacles"—Piercy, Marge. *Circles on the Water.* Knopf, 1982.

"Prospective Immigrants, Please Note"—Rich, Adrienne. *Collected Poems: 1950 to 2012.* W.W. Norton, 2016.

"I believe in all that has never yet been spoken"—Rilke, Rainer Maria. *Rilke's Book of Hours: Love Poems to God.* Translated by Anita Barrows and Joanna Marie Macy. Riverhead Books, 2005.

"I love the dark hours of my being"—Rilke, Rainer Maria. *Rilke's Book of Hours: Love Poems to God.* Translated by Anita Barrows and Joanna Marie Macy. Riverhead Books, 2005

"Lame Goat"—Rumi. In: Barks, Coleman. *The Essential Rumi.* HarperOne; Reissue expanded edition, 2004.

"Sky Circles"—Rumi. In: Barks, Coleman. *The Essential Rumi*. HarperOne; Reissue expanded edition, 2004.

"The Angels and The Furies"—Sarton, May. *Collected Poems, 1930–1993*. Open Road Media, 2014.

"Now I Become Myself"—Sarton, May. *Collected Poems, 1930–1993*. Open Road Media, 2014.

"You, Reading This Be Ready"—William Stafford. In Stafford, Kim, ed. *Ask Me: 100 Essential Poems by William Stafford*. Graywolf Press, 2014.

"Watching My Friend Pretend Her Heart Is Not Breaking"— Wahtola Trommer, Rosemerry, *All the Honey*, Samara Press, 2023.

"Love After Love"—Walcott, Derek. *Collected Poems, 1948–1984*. Farrar, Straus & Giroux, 1986.

"Sweet Darkness"—Whyte, David. *The House of Belonging*. Many Rivers Press, 1997.

"Start Close In"—Whyte, David. *David Whyte: Essentials*. Many Rivers Press, 2019.

EXPLORE POETS AND POETRY ORGANIZATIONS

The Academy of American Poets is responsible for Poem-a-Day, National Poetry Month, and an array of programs and educational resources. https://poets.org/

The League of Canadian Poets has a mandate is to elevate the cultural significance of poetry and champion the role of poets. Working to nurture and expand poetry communities and audiences, the organization cultivates the local, national, and international publication, performance, and recognition of poetry. The League supports equitable and inclusive artistic practice through poetry education and development. https://poets.ca/

The Poetry Coalition is an alliance of nearly 30 US organizations working together to promote the value poets bring to our culture and the important contribution poetry makes in the lives of people of all ages and backgrounds.

It is administered by The Academy of American Poets. https://poets.org/academy-american-poets/poetry-coalition

The Poetry Foundation is a place to discover more poets, poems, and resources, including in their Poem of the Day email and other newsletters. https://poetryfoundation.org

The Poetry Society, based in the United Kingdom, was founded in 1909 to promote "a more general recognition and appreciation of poetry." https://poetrysociety.org.uk/

Permission Credits

Acknowledgments

A big thank you:

To our friends who loved this idea and cheered us on.

To the poets from whom we received inspiration and windows into our memories and our hearts.

To Pádraig Ó Tuama, whose voice and sensibilities inspired us and whose curated book of poetry gifted us with "fresh eyes" to explore our lives.

To Parker Palmer, mentor, dear friend, and life-long teacher of living the undivided life—who set us on our way.

To Natalie Goldberg, whose writing practice teachings informed us always and held us steady when we hit a rough patch!

To Shelly, our knowledgeable, wise, appreciative editor, coach, guide, and friend on the journey and beyond (we couldn't have done it without her).

And each of us to each other in this partnered unfolding—a miracle and a joy.

Penny

To my dear partner David who supported and affirmed me every step of the way during the two years of writing this book and in life!

Darcy

To Shelley, my wife and partner in all things, who always gave me space to explore and discover.

To my sister Debbie, who looked out for me in the tough early years and has been a steady anchor ever since.

About the Authors

Penny Williamson, ScD, is an internationally recognized facilitator, educator, and coach for leaders in health care. She is a founding facilitator and mentor for the Center for Courage & Renewal and retired associate professor of medicine at the Johns Hopkins University School of Medicine. From 1998–2016, Penny led Courage to Lead, an 18-month national leadership development program for leaders in health care and other serving professions, based on the work of Parker J. Palmer and the Courage & Renewal approach. She has led workshops and retreats in the United States, Canada, the UK, Japan, Kenya, and Israel. Penny brings to her work an ecological worldview, and a belief in and attention to the inner life. Above all she brings a belief in the power of love and the capacity of individuals, groups, and organizations to contribute to creating a better world.

Darcy Shaw, DVM, MVSc, MBA, Diplomate ACVIM, is professor emeritus of small animal internal medicine at the Atlantic Veterinary College, University of Prince Edward Island, Canada. In his 40-plus years as a veterinarian, Darcy has worked as a clinician, an educator, held leadership positions, and contributed to multiple veterinary organizations in the US and Canada. He has participated in innovative leadership development programs such as Leading Organizations to

Health and Courage to Lead. Darcy is also a facilitator with the Center for Courage & Renewal and has offered retreats (Leading With Integrity) to leaders within the veterinary profession. Over his career, Darcy has developed profound appreciation for the dedication and compassion of those within the veterinary community, the power and sacredness of our relationship with animals, and the compelling need to find our own integrity and wholeness and see it in others.

About Creative Courage Press

Creative Courage Press is a small, independent publishing company founded in 2020 by Shelly L. Francis, inspired by the people she met while writing *The Courage Way: Leading and Living with Integrity* (Berrett-Koehler, 2018). Now, in collaboration with other authors, we are creating courage for the complexity of being human.

Get to know the essential voices of our remarkable authors and their refreshing ideas for leading change from the heart. Together we hope to generate meaningful conversations in our communities.

Visit us online to get fortified with resources and reflections for creating your own courageous way of life. As we grow, we invite you to grow with us.

www.CreativeCouragePress.com
hello@CreativeCouragePress.com

CREATIVE
COURAGE
PRESS

www.ingramcontent.com/pod-product-compliance
Lightning Source LLC
Chambersburg PA
CBHW031503120626
46545CB00005B/1720